IN FOCUS 1
ACADEMIC

A vocabulary-driven, multi-skills critical thinking course

Charles Browne • Brent Culligan • Joseph Phillips

KINSEIDO

Kinseido Publishing Co., Ltd.
3-21 Kanda Jimbo-cho, Chiyoda-ku,
Tokyo 101-0051, Japan

First published 2024 by Kinseido Publishing Co., Ltd.

Book and cover design SunCross Media LLC

Contents

Plan of the book

Unit	Title	Reading texts	Reading skills	Vocabulary	Listening
1 pp. 1–8	Gender Equality	1 The Iron Lady 2 What If Women Ruled the World?	Skimming Scanning Understanding the text Paraphrasing Making inferences	Definitions Word parts: *just/ju* Example: *justification*	Discussion dictation Listen to readings online
2 pp. 9–16	Marriage Around the World	1 Different Ways of Tying the Knot 2 Changing Views of Marriage	Skimming Scanning Understanding the text Making inferences Recognizing contrasts	Register Idioms with *break* Example: *break with tradition*	Discussion dictation Listen to readings online
3 pp. 17–24	A Thirsty World	1 The Cochabamba Water War 2 Water Worries	Skimming Scanning Understanding the text Reference words Making inferences	Definitions Word parts: *conscious* Example: *consciousness*	Discussion dictation Listen to readings online
4 pp. 25–32	Fished Out: Our Empty Oceans	1 The Grand Banks 2 Our Desert Oceans	Skimming Scanning Understanding the text Reference words Making inferences	Register Idioms with *turn* Example: *turn a blind eye*	Discussion dictation Listen to readings online
5 pp. 33–40	Nuclear Power: Clean and Bright	1 Green Energy? 2 The ONE Energy Solution	Skimming Scanning Understanding the text Recognizing contrasts Making inferences	Definitions Word parts: *trans* Example: *transmission*	Discussion dictation Listen to readings online
6 pp. 41–48	Renewable Energy: the Green Choice	1 Winds of Change 2 Beyond Fossil Fuels	Skimming Scanning Understanding the text Recognizing contrasts Making inferences	Register Phrasal verbs with *run* Example: *run out (of)*	Discussion dictation Listen to readings online

Research skills	Writing	Critical thinking	
		Skills	**Speaking**
Information gathering • Level of gender equality Interpreting and reporting results • Explaining differences	Writing a paragraph outline on the topic of women in power Topic sentence, main points, example	Identifying fact or assumption Completing a diagram: women in power	Discussion • New laws for gender equality Tip: Listening Quotable Quotes • Discussing the ways boys and girls are raised
Information gathering • Marriage and divorce by country Interpreting and reporting results • Explaining high and low divorce rates	Writing a paragraph Using types of reasoning to give a personal opinion about marriage	Identifying fact or assumption Understanding types of reasoning	Discussion • Pros and cons of arranged marriage Tip: Paraphrasing Quotable Quotes • Discussing love and marriage
Information gathering • Water resources and consumption by country Interpreting and reporting results • Explaining differences	Writing a paragraph Giving an opinion on the topic of water demand	Categorizing statements Completing a diagram: water demand	Presentation • Solutions to the world's water crisis Tip: Structuring your presentation Quotable Quotes • Globalization and access to safe water
Information gathering • Survey of fish stocks over time Interpreting and reporting results • Summarizing and explaining changes	Writing a paragraph Using types of reasoning to give a personal opinion about commercial fishing	Identifying fact or opinion Understanding types of reasoning	Role play and debate • Future fishing policy Tip: Voicing your opinion Quotable Quotes • Discussing the damaging effects of humans on the oceans
Information gathering • Two nuclear accidents Interpreting and reporting results • Comparing the accidents	Writing a paragraph Giving a personal opinion about the pros and cons of nuclear power	Identifying fact or opinion Completing a diagram: pros and cons of nuclear power	Role play and debate • Opinions about nuclear power Tip: Asking for opinions Quotable Quotes • Discussing energy sources and the politics of energy dependency
Information gathering • Changes in global energy sources Interpreting and reporting results • Discussing trends in energy supplies	Writing a paragraph Using facts and assumptions to give an opinion about renewable energy	Identifying fact or assumption Judging reasons	Presentation • The best renewable energy source for the future Tip: Openers Quotable Quotes • Discussing cheap fossil fuels and ways to promote renewable energy

Plan of the book

Unit	Title	Reading texts	Reading skills	Vocabulary	Listening
7 pp. 49–56	Free Trade: Cheap Goods or Good Jobs?	1 Free Trade in North America 2 Free Trade = No Bargain	Skimming Scanning Understanding the text Cause and effect Making inferences	Concordances Word parts: *capital* 　Example: *capitalist*	Discussion dictation Listen to readings online
8 pp. 57–64	Inequality in a Richer World	1 The Lehman Shock 2 The Promotion of Wealth	Skimming Scanning Understanding the text Cause and effect Making inferences	Collocations Idioms with *give* 　Example: *give the green light*	Discussion dictation Listen to readings online
9 pp. 65–72	Online Retailing: Disappearing Stores	1 The Disappearing Bookstore 2 The End of the Store as We Know It	Skimming Scanning Understanding the text Identifying reasons Recognizing bias	Concordances Idioms with *horse* 　Example: *back the wrong horse*	Discussion dictation Listen to readings online
10 pp. 73–80	The Office of the Future	1 COVID-19: Reshaping the Work-from-Home Landscape 2 Working from Home	Skimming Scanning Understanding the text Identifying reasons Recognizing bias	Collocations Phrasal verbs with *put* 　Example: *put up with*	Discussion dictation Listen to readings online
11 pp. 81–88	Online Addiction: Too Much Fun?	1 Internet Addiction 2 Fun, Popular, and Deadly	Skimming Scanning Understanding the text Identifying reasons Prediction: concluding statements	Concordances Phrasal verbs with *pass* 　Example: *pass away*	Discussion dictation Listen to readings online
12 pp. 89–96	Social Media: Changing Our Lives	1 The Unexpected Effects of Social Media 2 A Networked World	Skimming Scanning Understanding the text Paraphrasing Prediction: concluding statements	Collocations Phrasal verbs with *bring* 　Example: *bring about*	Discussion dictation Listen to readings online

Research skills	Writing	Critical thinking	
		Skills	**Speaking**
Information gathering • Global population, production, and trade over time Interpreting and reporting results • Analyzing trends	Writing a paragraph Giving a personal opinion about the pros and cons of free trade	Clarifying statements Completing a diagram: pros and cons of free trade	Discussion • Pros and cons of building a new factory Tip: Summarizing key points Quotable Quotes • Discussing equality and free trade
Information gathering • Income inequality by country Interpreting and reporting results • Comparing wealth and inequality	Writing a paragraph Using facts and opinions to give a personal opinion about capitalism	Clarifying statements Judging reasons	Discussion • Raising income tax to help the homeless and unemployed Tip: Interrupting Quotable Quotes • Comparing the goals of democratic governments with those of corporations
Information gathering • Growth in online shopping Interpreting and reporting results • Comparing trends by country	Writing a paragraph about the effects of showrooming Using types of reasoning	Identifying fact or assumption Understanding types of reasoning	Presentation • The effect of technology on the newspaper and travel industries Tip: Transition signals Quotable Quotes • Discussing the effect of the internet on publishing and other industries
Information gathering • Numbers of people working from home by education level and industry Interpreting and reporting results • Discussing remote working trends among employers	Writing a paragraph Describing the pros and cons of working from home and giving a personal opinion	Identifying cause and effect Judging reasons	Role play and debate • Whether a college should introduce e-learning Tip: Stressing keywords Quotable Quotes • Discussing job satisfaction and the balance between work and life activities
Information gathering • Video game facts and partner interview Interpreting and reporting results • Comparing and discussing results about gaming	Writing a letter to a newspaper Using types of reasoning to describe the negative effects of video games	Decision-making Understanding types of reasoning	Role play and debate • Government regulation and video games Tip: Disagreeing Quotable Quotes • Discussing the pros and cons of video games and TV
Information gathering • Numbers of users of popular social media sites Interpreting and reporting results • Explaining growth rates of different social media sites	Writing an email or a letter Making a recommendation about internet access at work or Saying what you plan to do about cyberbullying	Decision-making Judging reasons	Presentation • Cyberbullying and how to deal with it Tip: Closers Quotable Quotes • Discussing the impact of social media on people

Acknowledgments

Charles Browne would like to thank his wife, Yukari, and their three children, Joshua, Noah, and Hannah.

Joseph Phillips would like to acknowledge the support of his family.

Brent Culligan would like to thank his family in Japan and Canada who provided the motivation to take on this project.

The authors would like to thank Richard Walker for his tireless, patient, and positive support throughout the entire writing process.

The authors would also like to thank the entire Kinseido team for their faith in this exciting new chapter in the life of the *In Focus* series, especially Masato Fukuoka, Takahiro Imakado, Kyuta Sato and Alastair Lamond.

Kinseido and the authors appreciate Christopher Wenger and Brian Romeo of SunCross Media for their valuable design contributions.

To the teacher

Welcome to *In Focus*, a multi-level, corpus-informed course aimed at high school and university students. *In Focus* is designed to build all four skills while also systematically developing knowledge of core vocabulary and developing students' critical thinking skills. Each Student Book contains 12 topic-based units, which are divided into six general themes, providing two units in a row on each theme to help better develop students' critical thinking skills on these issues.

In Focus is supplemented by a range of free online learning components, which provide great flexibility and help to speed language acquisition.

We have created a unique lexical syllabus containing the most important words for second language learners of English. The authors of this series are also the creators of the New General Service List Project (www.newgeneralservicelist.com), a collection of corpus-based word lists, each providing the highest coverage in the world for that specific genre. The syllabus for *In Focus 1* and *In Focus 2* is based on the New General Service List (NGSL), a list of approximately 2,800 words that allows learners to understand approximately 92 percent of the words in most texts of general English. These are nearly all the words learners will ever need. The vocabulary syllabus for *In Focus Academic 1* is based on words from the New Academic Word List (NAWL), a list of approximately 960 words which, if learned in conjunction with the NGSL, provides approximately 92 percent coverage for most academic textbooks and lectures. In *In Focus Academic 1*, 120 of these words are taught in depth (10 per unit). Students can use the free online tools and resources developed especially for *In Focus* to learn additional unknown words from our NGSL and NAWL word lists.

All readings and written materials are graded to contain a very high percentage (90–95%) of high-frequency words from the NGSL and NAWL. This helps develop students' reading fluency and confidence.

Though *In Focus* can be used as a standalone textbook, dedicated online elements enable students to personalize and extend their learning beyond the classroom. Among the online components are interactive flashcards, interactive dictionaries that show the keywords being used in authentic video clips, crossword and word search puzzles, speed reading exercises, supplemental graded readings for each unit, vocabulary worksheets, and audio recordings of all reading texts.

In Focus Academic 1 follows on from *In Focus 1* and *In Focus 2*. It is designed for students at a high-intermediate level. Each unit is designed to help your students build both their knowledge as well as their ability to think critically about a wide range of important topics. The topics covered include gender equality, marriage around the world, renewable energy, nuclear power, free trade, online addiction, and the influence of social media. Language prompts are provided throughout to help students express themselves.

The *In Focus* Teacher's Manual contains full step-by-step teaching notes, unit-by-unit summaries, language notes, tips, extension activities, options for assessment, and a complete answer key.

We hope you and your students enjoy using *In Focus*.

Charles Browne   Brent Culligan   Joseph Phillips

How a unit works

All units in *In Focus* are eight pages long and follow a similar format. An audio icon reminds students they have the option of listening to the reading texts (available free from the website).

Unit organization

	Objective	Section
Page 1	Warm up Schema building Real-world connections	1 **Critical cartoons** Building knowledge Media link
Pages 2–3	Vocabulary development Reading Speaking	2 **Core vocabulary** Skimming and scanning Words in context: definitions; register; concordances; collocations Vocabulary building: idioms; word parts; phrasal verbs Discussion dictation
Pages 4–5	Reading Reading skills Speaking	3 **Reading skills** Pre-reading Reading Understanding the text; Paraphrasing; Making inferences; Recognizing contrasts; Reference words; Cause and effect; Identifying reasons; Recognizing bias; Prediction Discuss it
Page 6	Gathering, comparing, and analyzing information Speaking	4 **Researching a topic** Information gathering Interpreting and reporting results
Pages 7–8	Critical thinking skills Writing Discussion	5 **Critical thinking** Fact or assumption?; Categorizing; Fact or opinion?; Clarifying statements; Cause and effect; Decision-making Diagramming; Understanding reasoning; Judging reasons Writing Discussion; Presentation; Role play and debate Quotable Quotes

Unit sections

1 Critical cartoons

This is a short speaking activity centered on a cartoon related to the topic of the unit. All cartoons are authentic cartoons, and each was carefully chosen to represent the unit topic. Questions help activate schema and develop critical thinking skills.

2 Core vocabulary

Each unit teaches 10 important words from the New Academic Word List (NAWL). The section begins with a short reading passage (approximately 350 words) on an aspect of the unit topic that contextualizes the 10 keywords. A series of learning activities focuses on developing vocabulary knowledge, collocations, word parts, idioms, and phrasal verbs. This gives students practice using the words introduced in the unit. It also develops vocabulary learning skills and strategies that will be useful when encountering new words not introduced in the unit. A speaking activity rounds off this section.

3 Reading skills

Students work with a longer text (approximately 600 words) that gives a different or expanded point of view on the topic of the unit. This exposure to multiple points of view is a key aspect of developing skills in critical thinking. All 10 keywords appear in the second reading as well, providing additional in-context information about how the words are used. This is followed by a series of carefully structured activities, including pre-reading, comprehension, making inferences, and identifying opinions, facts, and assumptions. The section culminates in a short discussion.

4 Researching a topic

Since information from various points of view is crucial to thinking critically about an issue, the pair or group activities in this section encourage gathering further information related to the topic. This is followed by interpretation and presentation of the information collected.

5 Critical thinking

Through pair, group, and open class work, students are encouraged to develop critical thinking skills, such as identifying the difference between statements of fact and opinion, understanding different types of reasoning, analyzing charts and graphs, and categorizing data. Students then complete a writing task to express their opinion on the topic. The final page brings the content of the unit together in a discussion, presentation, or role play and debate about the topic. Presentation and discussion tips in each unit and useful language where necessary help students.

6 Quotable quotes

This final section introduces a quote on the topic of the unit by a famous person. Several thought-provoking questions on the quote conclude the unit. This section can be done in class as a short discussion activity or as a writing assignment outside the class.

To the student

Welcome to *In Focus*, a multi-level course for high school and university students. We have designed this series to help you build your vocabulary, work on all four basic skills (reading, writing, speaking, and listening), and help improve your discussion and presentation skills. *In Focus* will also help you think critically, which is a very important general academic skill. In each Student Book you will find 12 topic-based units. In addition to the Student Book, there is a range of free online components, which will help you focus on what you really need, learn more quickly, and become a more independent learner.

For *In Focus Academic 1*, we have created a unique vocabulary syllabus containing the most important academic vocabulary words for learners of English. This list has a total of about 960 words, which are nearly all the academic words you will ever need. If you know these words as well as our core list of 2,800 words, you will understand 92 percent of the words in most English academic texts and lectures. You will learn 120 of these words in each book, 10 per unit. You can use the website and online tools developed especially for *In Focus* to learn the rest of the words efficiently and enjoyably. Online, you will find a range of activities such as vocabulary puzzles, games, flashcards, and audio recordings of the reading texts.

In Focus Academic 1 follows on from *In Focus 1* and *In Focus 2*. It is designed for students at a high-intermediate level. Each unit will help you build your knowledge about a wide range of interesting topics as well as help you think critically about these topics. You will learn about and discuss topics such as gender equality, marriage around the world, renewable energy, nuclear power, free trade, online addiction, and the influence of social media. Four of the 12 units focus on discussion, four on presentation, and four on role play and debate. Each unit gives you a useful presentation or discussion tip to help you express yourself. In every unit, we also provide you with useful language and expressions where needed to help express yourself better.

We wish you good luck using *In Focus*. We are sure that the book and the online materials will help you to learn English quickly and in a fun way!

Charles Browne

Brent Culligan

Joseph Phillips

In this unit, you will:
- read an article about a female British prime minister.
- read an article about women and power.
- discuss gender-equality laws in your country.

1 Critical cartoons

A Building knowledge

Work with a partner or in a small group. Look at the information on this page and the cartoon. Discuss the questions below.

1 A "glass ceiling" is an invisible barrier for people trying to advance in their careers. It often affects women and minorities. Are there any glass ceilings in your country?

2 Has a woman been the leader of your country or of a major company in your country?

3 Do you think opportunities for women are equal to men in your country? Why or why not?

4 What is the message of the cartoon? What is the connection to the unit topic?

> I think there is a glass ceiling in ...

> We have (never) had a woman as leader of ...

> I think opportunities for women are ...

> I think the cartoon is making the point that ...

MEDIA link *The Eagle Huntress* (2016) is a beautifully filmed documentary about a 13-year-old Mongolian girl who, with the help of her father, tries to become the first female eagle hunter in her country.

For additional media links, go to infocus-eltseries.com

2 Core vocabulary

A Skimming and scanning

1 Find and underline the keywords in the text. Try to guess their meanings.

Keywords

authority	discrimination	distribution	dominant	ethical
justification	motive	scenario	traditionally	unstable

The Iron Lady

What would happen if more women were in positions of power? Would governments be any different if women had the authority to start wars, set economic policy, and run countries? In 1979, Margaret Thatcher took power in the United Kingdom. She belonged to a political party that was traditionally run by white males. Many of its party members believed that women belonged in the kitchen and not in the government. Thatcher overcame discrimination in her own political party to become its first female leader. She then went on to become Britain's first female prime minister and was a dominant   5
political force in the 1980s.

Her first major test came in 1982, when the Argentinian military attacked some small islands claimed by both countries. These were the Falkland Islands, known as the Malvinas in Argentina. Though Argentina had many motives for the attack, it is possible that it thought a woman would be less likely to go to war. Its generals felt that the most likely scenario was for Thatcher to go to the United Nations. They were wrong. The prime minister sent the British military to retake the islands and it defeated the   10
Argentinian forces.

Two years later, Thatcher began some of the most controversial policies in British history. When she took power, Britain's economy was unstable and there were many problems. Some industries needed support from the government because they were losing money. But she thought that taxing rich people and giving the money to other   15
people was like stealing and not ethical. She didn't support the government's role in income distribution. This led to her fighting many battles with the labor unions. She closed or sold many weaker state-owned companies. Her justification was that support for dying industries hurt the country's economic growth. Naturally, this resulted in the loss of many jobs. Although the economy finally began to improve,   20
many British working people grew to hate the "Iron Lady," as she became known.

So, was Margaret Thatcher's government different because she was a woman? If she is a good example of a female politician, it seems true to say that a politician's actions are influenced more by his or her beliefs than being male or female.

2 Read the titles below. Which would also be a good title for the text? Circle A, B, or C. Then explain your answer to a partner.

   A Britain's First Female Prime Minister

   B Margaret Thatcher and the Unions

   C Margaret Thatcher's Economic Policies

B Words in context: definitions

1 Look at the definitions of the three keywords below. Find the definition that matches how each word is used in the text on **page 2**.

distribution   **1**   the process of giving things out to people, or spreading or supplying something
            2   the way in which people or things are spread out in a place

unstable   **1**   describes someone who suffers from sudden and extreme changes of mental state
            2   not firm and therefore not strong, safe, or likely to last

authority   **1**   an expert on a subject
            2   a group of people with official responsibility for a particular area of activity
            3   moral or legal right or ability to control

2 Make your own sentences using the keywords and compare them with a partner. Which meanings does your partner use?

1 _____

2 _____

3 _____

C Vocabulary building: word parts: *just/ju*   Example: *justification*

Words with *just/ju*

judge	jury	justify	justification	unjust

1 Use the words in the box to complete the sentences below. Try to guess the meaning of any words you don't know.

1 Maria tried to _____ her poor performance in the tennis tournament by blaming her new coach.

2 There was no _____ for his rude behavior.

3 Many people consider that Nelson Mandela's imprisonment was _____.

4 Thurgood Marshall was the first African-American Supreme Court _____.

5 A _____ can have as few as six or as many as 12 members.

2 Work with a partner. What do you think *just/ju* means? Write your guess below. Then check your answer with another partner.

I think *just/ju* means _____

D Discussion dictation

1 Listen and write down the questions. Then discuss them in small groups.

1 _____ ?

2 _____ ?

3 _____ ?

2 Form new groups and compare your answers.

3 Reading skills

A Pre-reading

1 Quickly scan the text and circle the 10 keywords.

2 Why are there so few women in positions of power in the world? Give two reasons.

3 Which of these countries do you think has the largest proportion of female company directors: the United States, Germany, or Norway?

B Reading

Read the text and check your answers to the pre-reading questions above. Then highlight an interesting idea in each paragraph.

What If Women Ruled the World?

In most countries, women are poorly represented in positions of leadership and authority. In government, for example, there are relatively few women and only one country, Rwanda, has had a majority of females
5 in the national parliament. Developed countries are often far down on the scale of female representation in government. Of 188 countries, Britain ranks 47th, with 35 percent, and the United States 71st, with 29 percent. In Asia, South Korea comes 131st, with 18
10 percent, and Japan 164th, with only 10 percent female representation.

Women's representation in corporate boardrooms is no better: men are again dominant. In the United States, only 31 percent of board members are women.
15 In Europe, things are a little better with 44 percent in Germany, 40 percent in Italy and the UK, 36 percent in Sweden and 35 percent in Spain. In Asia things are generally worse, with only 24 percent in Singapore and 12 percent in Japan, for example.

20 The relatively high figures for female leaders in Rwanda and Germany can be explained by the fact that in these countries, there are laws that require a minimum percentage of women in government and business. The justification for laws such as these is
25 fairness, but are there any other reasons to encourage greater participation of women in positions of power? There are five reasons for the answer to this question being a clear yes.

First, when selecting the best people for government,
30 management, or any other field, it makes sense to have the widest possible choice. The United States and China win most Olympic medals largely because they can recruit from the largest populations. Since women make up half the population, it makes sense
35 to draw on their talents to the same degree as those of men.

Second, the background and experience of women mean that they have insights that are often lacking in men. As the primary caregivers to children and
40 the elderly, they are traditionally more likely to push for improvement in the areas of social welfare and education. Similarly, as more frequent victims

of discrimination than men, women tend to be more sympathetic to minorities and the oppressed. Often mothers and grandmothers, women usually take a long-term view and consider the welfare of future generations. With climate change and the threat of an unstable future, this long-term view is exactly what is needed in leadership.

Third, women are often more likely than men to have peace as a motive for their actions. Mothers, who make a huge investment in their children, are generally less willing to send those children to war. Figures show that as many as 175 million people died in wars and revolutions in the twentieth century. Would this number be as shockingly high if women had held more positions of political power?

Fourth, women have a stronger tendency than men to avoid risk and pursue compromise. The financial crisis of 2008 was largely due to risk-taking by male financial managers. Had the world's fourth-largest investment bank been Lehman Sisters instead of Lehman Brothers, would we have experienced the same scenario?

Finally, women are often superior managers to men. As the main caregivers and managers of family affairs, women have to be highly organized. They are natural multitaskers. These skills are exactly what is required to successfully manage a company or public policy.

For all these reasons, it is time that the distribution of power in the world shifted in favor of women to better reflect their numbers in the population. This is the right thing to do, not just for ethical reasons, but also because it will result in a better world for all.

C Understanding the text

Read the questions below and circle the correct answers according to the text.

1 **GIST** What is this text mainly about?
   - **A** Women and discrimination
   - **B** Women and power
   - **C** Women and politics

2 **MAIN IDEA** Which of the following statements best describes the main idea of the text?
   - **A** Women face discrimination in all areas of life.
   - **B** It is a fact that women are more capable than men in all areas.
   - **C** There are several good reasons for giving women more power.

3 **DETAILS** There are more female company board members in Germany because …
   - **A** German law requires a certain proportion of women.
   - **B** Germany has more educated women than other European countries.
   - **C** German women are naturally powerful.

4 **DETAILS** If more women were in power, there would probably be fewer wars because …
   - **A** women are better managers than men.
   - **B** women are more interested in education and welfare than men.
   - **C** women as mothers do not want their children to be killed.

D Paraphrasing

> **paraphrasing**
> stating something spoken or written in a shorter and simpler form

The statements below paraphrase the author's points of view. In each case, identify the paragraph that best matches the statement.

1 As mothers and daughters, women often have a greater understanding of welfare issues. _____
2 Women's experience in household management makes them better candidates for leadership in government and business. _____
3 Wealthy countries have surprisingly few women in executive positions in business. _____
4 To find the best people possible, candidates should be selected on their skills. _____
5 Men take more unnecessary risks than women, so women make better leaders. _____
6 Wealthy countries have surprisingly few women in government. Fairness is only one reason women should be more represented in society. _____
7 Women as leaders are less likely to engage in conflicts. _____

E Making inferences

Which one of the following statements by Margaret Thatcher would the author of the text most strongly agree with? Circle the correct answer. Then compare your answers with a partner.

1 "The battle for women's rights has been largely won."
2 "Any woman who understands the problems of running a home will be nearer to understanding the problems of running a country."
3 "In politics, if you want anything said, ask a man. If you want anything done, ask a woman."
4 "I've got a woman's ability to stick to a job and get on with it when everyone else walks off and leaves it."

Discuss it

Work with a partner or in a small group. Ask and answer the questions below.
1 Look back at the ideas you highlighted. Are they the same? What are the differences?
2 The author describes improvements in some areas of life if more women occupied positions of power. What other things would be different if women had more power?
3 Are there any roles or types of jobs that should be performed only by women or only by men?

4 Researching a topic

A Information gathering

The Global Gender Gap Index is an indicator of the level of gender equality in a country. The index goes from 0 to 1. A score of 1 means women and men are equal.

Work with a partner. One is Student A; one is Student B. Student A: use the table below. Student B: use the table on page 97. Ask your partner for the missing information and complete the table.

Global Gender Gap Index (total of 146 countries)					
Rank	Country	Score	Rank	Country	Score
	Afghanistan	0.41	33	Mexico	
36		0.76	116	Nepal	0.66
57	Brazil	0.73	2		0.88
30	Canada	0.77	142	Pakistan	0.58
	China	0.68	12	Rwanda	0.79
3	Finland	0.86	131	Saudi Arabia	0.64
	Iceland	0.91	49	Singapore	0.74
127	India			South Korea	0.68
87	Indonesia	0.70	18		0.79
11		0.80	5	Sweden	0.82
79	Italy	0.71	48	Tanzania	0.74
	Japan	0.65	129	Turkey	0.64
82	Lesotho		71	United Arab Emirates	
102	Malaysia	0.68	43	United States	0.75

Source: World Economic Forum, Global Gender Gap Index, 2023

B Interpreting and reporting results

1 Work in small groups. Discuss the questions below.

  1 What trends in the data can you identify?

  2 What unexpected data did you find? Give reasons for your answers.

  3 Do you think it is possible for a country to achieve a score of 1 ? Give reasons.

  4 The Global Gender Gap Index considers four areas: economic participation, education, health, and politics. Which do you think is most important? Why?

2 Share your group's ideas with the class.

There is a clear correlation between ... and ...

In our view, it would only be possible to ... if ...

We were really surprised that ... because ...

One possible reason for this is ...

5 Critical thinking

A Fact or assumption?

Below is part of a speech by a senior female politician. Work with a partner and decide if her promises are based on facts (F) or assumptions (A).

1 First, I promise to make two years of university education free for everyone. Our investment in education for our young people today is an investment in a rich future tomorrow. _____

2 Second, I promise to reduce the size of the armed forces. The Cold War is over, and we have no obligation to become the world's police force. _____

3 Finally, I promise to manage the national budget efficiently. As a mother and household manager, I am an expert on budgets. _____

B Diagramming

Work in small groups. Below is a diagram showing the possible consequences of women having more power. Add your own ideas to the diagram. Add boxes as necessary. You may want to refer to the text on page 4.

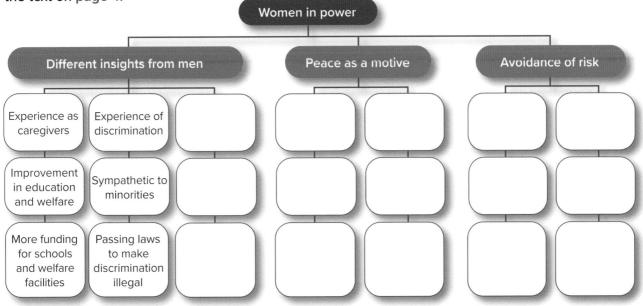

C Writing

The diagram has notes for three topic sentences:

1 Women often have different insights from men.

2 Women are more likely than men to have peace as a motive for their actions.

3 Women have a stronger tendency than men to avoid risk.

topic sentence
a sentence that explains the main idea or ideas of a paragraph. It is often the first sentence of the paragraph.

Each of these parts might correspond to a paragraph in a short essay on women in power. Choose one topic sentence from your completed diagram and write an outline for a paragraph. An example is shown below.

Topic sentence	Women often have different or better insights than men.
Main point 1	One reason for women's different insights is that they often have experience as caregivers.
Detail	This can lead to improvement in education and welfare.
Example	An example of this improvement is more funding for schools and welfare facilities.

D Discussion

Norway is a progressive country when it comes to gender equality. Norway also has these two laws:

1 Forty percent of the directors of public companies in Norway must be women.
2 Women can be drafted into the Norwegian military in the same way as men.

1 A new government wants to pass similar laws in your country. Work in small groups. Group A: think of reasons to support the proposed laws. Group B: think of reasons to oppose the proposed laws. Choose A or B. Use the table to help you organize your ideas.

| | Things to consider | |
Proposed new law	In favor	Against
1 Forty percent of the directors of public companies must be women.	Economy Effect on company staff Fairness Gender equality Talent pool	Government control Expense Fairness Implementation issues Selection made on gender versus talent
2 Women can be drafted into the military and fight in the same way as men.	Fairness Equality Talent pool	Gender differences Effect on military Effect on men and cost

2 Form new groups. Students from Group A should join students from Group B. Share your ideas. Ask follow-up questions and explain your reasoning.

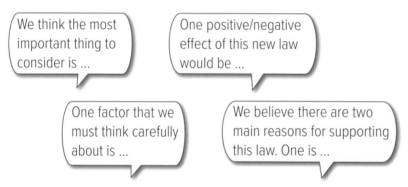

We think the most important thing to consider is …

One positive/negative effect of this new law would be …

One factor that we must think carefully about is …

We believe there are two main reasons for supporting this law. One is …

> **TIP**
>
> **Listening**
> Remember to listen carefully to what the other person says. If you only think about what you are going to say, you may miss the important parts of a discussion. We learn by listening to the other side of the argument. It is also important to show the speaker you are listening. Make eye contact and provide regular feedback to show you understand, for example by nodding or using short expressions, such as *I see* or *uh-huh*.

3 Who has the strongest arguments? Vote on each proposal as a class. Would the proposals succeed or fail in becoming law?

Quotable quotes
Final thoughts …

We've begun to raise daughters more like sons … but few have the courage to raise our sons more like our daughters.

Gloria Steinem
American journalist and social activist

1 Explain the quote in your own words. Does it need courage to do what Gloria Steinem suggests?

2 What are some ways girls and boys are raised differently in your country?

3 Should parents raise girls and boys differently? Why or why not?

In this unit, you will:

- read an article about marriage customs.
- read an article about changing views of marriage.
- discuss the pros and cons of arranged marriages.

1 Critical cartoons

A Building knowledge

Work with a partner or in a small group. Look at the information on this page and the cartoon. Discuss the questions below.

1 What do you think is important for a successful marriage or partnership?

2 What things do you think can cause problems in a relationship?

3 How have marriage customs changed in your country over the last 50 years?

4 What is the message of the cartoon? What is the connection to the unit topic?

> One thing I think is important is ...

> I imagine ... could cause problems in a relationship.

> One thing that has changed about marriage is ...

> I think the cartoon is trying to tell us ...

MEDIA link

Love Around the World (2021) is a documentary filmed by a newly-married couple from Croatia, who go on a 15-month journey around the world. The film shows 33 different stories about love and marriage.

For additional media links, go to infocus-eltseries.com

A Skimming and scanning

1 Find and underline the keywords in the text. Try to guess their meanings.

Keywords

| breakdown | compensate | elimination | formally | genetic(s) |
| goods | historically | legitimate | punishment | viable |

Different Ways of Tying the Knot

Marriage is a custom that is found in many variations and in all societies. It is influenced by both genetic and social factors. Though people often believe that the way marriage is practiced in their culture is the only viable arrangement, there are different ways for people to be married, and these have changed over time. A major distinction is between monogamy (mono meaning "one"), which describes a marriage to only one person at a time, and polygamy (poly

5   meaning "many"), in which a person may marry more than one person at a time.

With monogamy, it used to be common for one family to compensate the other with money, property, or goods. When the bride's family compensates the groom in this way, it is called a dowry. Because of the financial burden on the bride's family, many countries have broken with this tradition, and dowries are illegal in some places where they were once common, for example, India. Another big change in marriage customs is with the ending of a marriage. Up until the

10   twentieth century, very few people could get a divorce. When this became easier, some people predicted a breakdown in society. Luckily, that hasn't happened.

Within polygamy, there are marriages in which a husband can have two or more wives or marriages in which a

15   wife can have two or more husbands. Both have been legitimate forms of marriage at one time or another in different cultures. For example, the Mormons in the United States practiced polygamy until it was made illegal in 1862. Despite the threat of punishment, some groups

20   there continue to practice polygamy, and its elimination from North America is far from certain. In Africa and across

the Middle East, there are many countries today where polygamy is legal. Historically, there are far fewer examples of women having more than one husband, and no countries today formally recognize this type of polygamy. It was a common practice in ancient Sparta (part of modern-day Greece), and it may still be practiced informally today in parts of

25   Tibet, where the usual practice is for brothers to share one wife and so help keep the family property undivided.

2 Read the titles below. Which would also be a good title for the text? Circle A, B, or C. Then explain your answer to a partner.

A In Defense of Traditional Marriage

B Types of Polygamy

C Marriage around the World

B Words in context: register

synonym
a word or phrase that has the same or nearly the same meaning as another word or phrase

1 "Register" refers to the degree of formality in language. Match the keyword in each sentence below from the text to its synonym. The synonyms are less formal than the keywords.

   1 When the bride's family **compensates** the groom in this way, it is called a dowry.

     A charges

     B pays

     C tells

   2 Both have been **legitimate** forms of marriage at one time or another in different cultures.

     A fake

     B happy

     C real

   3 Its **elimination** from North America is far from certain.

     A removal

     B spread

     C influence

2 Now rewrite in your own words each of the sentences above using the less formal synonym. Where possible, match the tone of the sentence to the synonym.

   1 _____

   2 _____

   3 _____

C Vocabulary building: idioms   Example: *break with tradition*

1 Below are some idioms with the word *break*. Match each idiom to its meaning.

idiom
a group of words that together have a meaning that is different from the meanings of the separate words

break with tradition	to give someone important new information
break even	to make people feel relaxed with each other, often by starting a conversation
break the news	to get the same amount as that invested in a business
break the ice	to do something different from what is usual

2 Complete the sentences below with the correct idiom.

   1 The record company decided to _____ and release the album for free.

   2 After two years in business, Kate's Muffin Shop is just beginning to _____.

   3 She couldn't wait to _____ about her job offer to her boyfriend.

   4 A short self-introduction is a good way to _____ at a business convention.

3 Now use the idioms to make your own sentences.

D Discussion dictation

1 Listen and write down the questions. Then discuss them in small groups.

   1 _____ ?

   2 _____ ?

   3 _____ ?

2 Form new groups and compare your answers.

A Pre-reading

1 Quickly scan the text and circle the 10 keywords.

2 What are two traditional functions of marriage?

3 Approximately what percentage of women in the United States have lived with a partner without being married?

A 10 percent   **B** 25 percent   **C** 50 percent   **D** 60 percent

B Reading

Read the text and check your answers to the pre-reading questions above. Then highlight an interesting idea in each paragraph.

Changing Views of Marriage

Marriage is a truly universal concept. In fact, there is no culture in the world in which some form of marriage doesn't exist. The form that marriage takes may vary greatly from place to place, but if we look at the social
5 functions behind marriage, we see many similarities.

Historically, marriage has had four main functions. First, there are rules as to who can marry, and these rules usually prohibit marriage between close relatives. The science of genetics in the twentieth
10 century has demonstrated that this promotes the elimination of health problems that can occur in children of such marriages.

The second function of traditional marriage has been to protect the property and inheritance rights of
15 children. Until recently, marriage ceremonies were always public, and children of the marriage were publicly recognized as having these rights. Children born outside a marriage often had no such rights.

The third function of marriage is to protect the rights of
20 women. Historically, in a majority of societies around the world, women had few, if any, rights. In particular, they had no property rights. Beyond clothes and other personal items, they owned few goods and depended on their husbands for everything. Customs associated
25 with marriage compensated for this lack of rights and provided some protection for women who were divorced or widowed.

A final function of marriage has been to preserve the unity of a particular group. This group might be
30 linked by religion or race. Many cultures have had traditions that prohibit marriage outside the dominant religion. Similarly, in some cultures, marriage to
35 someone of a different race has been prohibited and even criminalized. In the United States, for example, until the Supreme Court ruled it illegal in 1967, 16
40 states had laws that prohibited interracial marriage. Participants in such marriages were subject to punishment as criminals. Another way to maintain group unity has been through arranged marriages, sometimes of children; this has been common in societies where group identity is seen as important.

Some countries still maintain institutions that support part or all of these traditional functions of marriage. However, over the last 100 years or so, especially in Western countries, there has been a shift away from strict observance of rules that preserve these functions. This is because the conditions that gave rise to these functions of marriage have changed. Marriage is no longer the only evidence of fatherhood. Genetic testing can easily prove who a child's legitimate father is. Similarly, the rights of women, especially property rights, are increasingly protected by law, and in many cases, women no longer need to be married to claim these rights. Furthermore, laws that prohibited marriage between different racial or ethnic groups no longer exist in most countries. And with globalization and massive immigration around the world, interracial marriage is no longer unusual in many countries.

Are we perhaps seeing a trend that is leading toward the breakdown of traditional marriage? It is true that in many parts of the world, traditional marriage is still the norm, but it seems that with economic progress comes the liberalization of society. As children, women, and minorities receive greater legal protection and equality, marriage is undergoing a transformation. More and more couples are living together without formally recognizing their relationship through marriage. In the United States, for example, nearly half of all women between 15 and 44 have experienced such a union. Another example of this transformation is same-sex marriage. In 2013, the United States Supreme Court struck down as illegal a federal law that defined marriage as being between a man and a woman. These recent trends suggest that at least in some countries, traditional marriage between a man and a woman is no longer the only viable option. However, that doesn't mean that traditional marriage will cease to be the norm anytime soon.

C Understanding the text

Read the questions below and circle the correct answers according to the text.

1 GIST What is this text mainly about?

    A The breakdown of marriage

    B Traditional views of marriage

    C Marriage then and now

2 MAIN IDEA Which of the following statements best describes the main idea of the text?

    A Marriage has protected the rights of women and children.

    B Marriage customs vary a lot depending on the country and culture.

    C The reasons for marriage have changed, especially in Western countries.

3 DETAILS Until 1967, people of different races who married in some US states could ...

    A be arrested.

    B not be married in a church.

    C be accused of marrying outside their religion.

4 DETAILS Which one of the following has not been a function of traditional marriage?

    A Protection of women's rights

    B Protection of children's rights

    C Protection of the rights of minorities

D Making inferences

Which two of the following sentences could the author have written?

1 Traditional marriage will disappear within 50 years.

2 Couples should be encouraged to marry rather than live together.

3 Marriage is changing in societies all over the world.

4 In the future, perhaps most couples will live together without being married.

5 As countries develop economically, traditional marriage will become less important.

E Recognizing contrasts

1 The words *however* and *but* are often used to describe contrasting ideas. Scan the text for these words and summarize the contrasting ideas in each case.

	Idea 1	Idea 2
1 (Paragraph 1)	_____ , but	_____.
2 (Paragraph 6)	_____ ; however,	_____.
3 (Paragraph 7)	_____ , but	_____.
4 (Paragraph 7)	_____ ; however,	_____.

2 Work with a partner. Take turns explaining the ideas in each case in your own words.

Discuss it

Work with a partner or in a small group. Ask and answer the questions below.

1 Look back at the ideas you highlighted. Are they the same? What are the differences?

2 If fewer people marry in the future, how will this affect society? Think about population changes, children, homes.

3 Do you think the changing nature of marriage in some countries is positive or negative? Why? In what ways?

A Information gathering

Below is a table on marriage and divorce rates in countries around the world. Work with a partner. One is Student A; one is Student B. Student A: use the table below. Student B: use the table on page 97. Ask your partner for the missing information and complete the table.

Marriage and divorce rates around the world			
Country	Marriage rate (per 1,000)	Divorce rate (per 1,000)	Marriages ending in divorce
Brazil		1.4	21%
China	7.2	3.2	
Egypt	11.0		17%
Iran	11.2	1.6	
Italy		1.5	47%
Japan	4.8	1.7	
Russia		3.9	74%
South Korea	4.7		47%
Turkey		1.7	25%
United States	5.1	2.3	

Source: Wikipedia

B Interpreting and reporting results

1 Work in small groups. Discuss the questions below.

    1 Which countries have the highest divorce rates?

    2 Which countries have the lowest marriage rates?

    3 What social, cultural, or other factors might explain the values in the data?

    4 How does your country compare? Try to find the marriage and divorce rates for your country if it is not on the list.

2 Share your group's ideas with the class. What factors did you identify? Which are most important?

We thought that ... countries were similar because ...

In our group, we suggested that the low divorce rate in ... might be explained by ...

We think that countries that ... generally have lower divorce rates.

One factor that may influence divorce rates is ...

5 Critical thinking

A Fact or assumption?

There are many different points of view on the subject of marriage. Work with a partner and decide if the following statements are based on facts (F) or assumptions (A).

1 The older couples are when they marry, the less likely they are to divorce.   _____

2 Legalization of same-sex marriage will lead to a fall in birthrates.   _____

3 If people are made to live together before marriage, they are less likely to divorce.   _____

4 Women have their first child at an older age than they did 50 years ago.   _____

5 A traditional marriage, in which the husband works and the wife raises the children, is the most stable.   _____

B Understanding reasoning

It is important to understand the different types of reasoning used in discussions. Four of the most important types are defined below. Read the definitions and then do the exercise that follows.

Cause and effect states why something happens (the cause) and what happens as a result (the effect).
Conditional states that if one thing is true then another is also likely to be true.
Comparative states that a conclusion can be drawn by comparing different ideas or situations.
Pros and cons states arguments for and against a proposal.

1 Jessica and Brendan are discussing marriage. What types of reasoning do they use? Identify the types and underline the words that support your answers.

Type of reasoning

Jessica: Because women's rights are protected, marriage has lost much of its meaning.   _____

Brendan: Do you really think so? I think marriage still has a purpose. For example, if a couple has an arranged marriage, they are less likely to divorce.   _____

Jessica: Marriage may provide a stable environment for children, but it limits personal freedom.   _____

Brendan: Well, religion is important, too. The divorce rate is lower in countries where religion is strong than in countries where people are not religious.   _____

2 Compare your answers with a partner.

C Writing

Look at the statements in A and B above. Write a paragraph that expresses your opinion about the value of marriage. Try to use at least two of the types of reasoning. Then compare your paragraph with a partner.

D Discussion

You are going to discuss the pros and cons of arranged marriage. Customs vary, but the main features of arranged marriage are that the decision involves more people than the couple, and that both sides agree to the marriage.

1 Form small groups. Choose A or B.

Group A: discuss the advantages of arranged marriages.

Group B: discuss the disadvantages of arranged marriages.

Think about the families involved and the married couple. The following factors may help you.

age difference	looks	physical attraction
compatibility	money	profession
divorce rate	personal choice	romantic love
family background	personality	success
interests		

2 Form new groups. Students from Group A should join students from Group B. Compare your ideas and discuss the different points of view. Use the types of reasoning you have learned.

3 Share your ideas with the class. Overall, do you think arranged marriage is a good idea?

> The main reason we think arranged marriages are good / bad is that ...

> We agreed that arranged marriages have several good points, but ...

> One way arranged marriage may be good is ... but ...

> If a couple's marriage is arranged, then one disadvantage is ...

TIP

Paraphrasing
When explaining or sharing ideas with others, it is helpful to summarize your thoughts with simpler statements. This is called paraphrasing. You can use the expressions below to paraphrase.

Simply put, what I'm trying to say is ...
Basically, we think that ...
In a nutshell, our view is that ... because ...

66 Quotable quotes
Final thoughts ... 99

Where there's marriage without love, there will be love without marriage.

Benjamin Franklin
Founding Father of the United States

1 Explain in your own words what Franklin means.

2 Do you agree with this quote? Why or why not?

3 How is this quote connected to the topic of this unit?

A Thirsty World

In this unit, you will:
- read an article about a water war.
- read an article about global water shortages.
- discuss and make a presentation on solutions to water issues.

1 Critical cartoons

A Building knowledge

Work with a partner or in a small group. Look at the information on this page and the cartoon. Discuss the questions below.

1 Does your country face any challenges regarding water? If so, what?

2 What illnesses or diseases can be caused by drinking dirty water?

3 Poorer countries have many needs besides water. What are some common issues?

4 What is the message of the cartoon? What is the connection to the unit topic?

> In my country, sometimes we have the problem of ...

> I think ... is caused by drinking dirty water.

> One issue that less-developed countries face is ...

> I think this cartoon is highlighting the fact that ...

MEDIA link

Brave Blue World (2020) is a hopeful documentary about the world water crisis. Narrated by Liam Neeson and featuring Matt Damon, it tells the stories of people facing water challenges, and it explores solutions to the problem.

For additional media links, go to infocus-eltseries.com

A Skimming and scanning

1 Find and underline the keywords in the text. Try to guess their meanings.

Keywords

consciousness	consumption	emergence	evident	minimal
namely	norm	prevalence	publish	ridiculous

The Cochabamba Water War

In 2000, a curious event happened in Cochabamba, Bolivia, that started a worldwide debate about the ownership of water. Water isn't like other goods. It is a necessity. Though we can survive on minimal amounts of water, we usually need about two liters a day. We can use more water when it is cheap, but we can't cut our consumption below this amount if the price goes up. Throughout most of history, water has been free, where available. Making sure that people had enough

5 water was one of the duties of a ruler. The emergence of cities some 7,000 years ago was marked by the beginnings of waterworks, and the prevalence of fountains in ancient cities shows us just how important water was.

Then, in 1999, this norm was challenged. The government of Bolivia was faced with a huge debt. It turned to the World Bank for help, which advised it to sell a number

10 of public services, namely railroads, telephone services, and airlines. In a document published in 2002, the World Bank admitted to advising Bolivia to sell the Cochabamba water service. The sale took place in 1999. It soon became evident that, under the terms of the sale, the company

15 that bought the water utility had the rights to water that had traditionally been free: water from rivers and even from rainwater. The company made a promise to the government that it would make many improvements. To meet its promise, the company raised water rates by 35 percent. Poor people couldn't afford this increase. For many such

20 people, it seemed ridiculous that the company could cut off water to their homes. Local people began a protest in 2000 that became known as the Cochabamba Water War, and it soon gained worldwide attention. The protests raised world consciousness about how companies were taking advantage of people in poor countries. Finally, after months of protests and riots, the water service was returned to the local government's control.

2 Read the statements below. Which best summarizes the text? Circle A, B, or C. Then explain your answer to a partner.

A Large corporations can supply water to towns more efficiently.

B The World Bank gives good advice for fixing a country's economic problems.

C Selling the rights to provide water services to companies is not always a good idea.

B Words in context: definitions

1 Look at the definitions of the two keywords below. Find the definition that matches how each word is used in the text on page 18.

consciousness
1 the state of understanding and realizing something
2 the state of being awake, thinking, and knowing what is happening around you

publish
1 to produce and sell a book, magazine, or newspaper
2 to make information available to the public, especially in a book, newspaper, magazine, etc.

2 Make your own sentences using the keywords and compare them with a partner. Which meanings does your partner use?

1 _____

2 _____

C Vocabulary building: word parts: *conscious*   Example: *consciousness*

Words with *conscious*

conscious	consciousness	self-conscious	subconscious	unconscious

1 Use the words in the box to complete the sentences below. Try to guess the meaning of any words you don't know.

1 The accident victim was still _____ when paramedics reached her.

2 Victor felt _____ when asked to sing at Ben's birthday party.

3 Lan hit her head on a tree branch and was knocked _____ for a few minutes.

4 The psychiatrist suggested that I had a _____ fear of speaking in public.

5 It's time to raise people's _____ on the issue of bottled water.

2 Work with a partner. What do you think *conscious* means? Write your guess below. Then check your answer with another partner.

I think *conscious* means _____.

D Discussion dictation

1 Listen and write down the questions. Then discuss them in small groups.

1 _____ ?

2 _____ ?

3 _____ ?

2 Form new groups and compare your answers.

3 Reading skills

A Pre-reading

1 Quickly scan the text and circle the 10 keywords.

2 What are two problems relating to water that people face in the world?

3 Which countries might face water problems in the future?

B Reading

Read the text and check your answers to the pre-reading questions above. Then highlight an interesting idea in each paragraph.

Water Worries

If you live in the developed world, it's something you probably don't think about. It's always there, it's always been there, and it always will be there. Clean water available everywhere at a minimal cost is something
5 that we have come to take for granted. But regrettably, this is not the norm, and countless people in the world do not have the luxury of thinking in this way. There are two main problems that people face relating to water. First, for many, there is a scarcity of water.
10 There just isn't enough of it. For many more, water may be available, but it isn't clean enough for drinking, cooking, or bathing.

Water scarcity is a critical problem now and is likely to get worse in the future. China is a good example
15 of a country that is facing serious water problems. Since the 1950s, China has lost 28,000 rivers. They have dried up because the water has been used for industry or agriculture. Much of the north of China is dry, and yet cities with populations of more than
20 one million people have been built there. China has constructed a huge canal system that pumps water from rivers in the south of China to the arid north. Environmentalists, along with those who depend on the river for their livelihood, such as fishermen and
25 farmers, are against this.

In many areas of the world where water is available, it is often undrinkable and sometimes even dangerous to bathe in. There are two reasons for this. The first is that in developing countries, rivers often function
30 as sewers. Human waste goes directly into the river with minimal or no treatment, and the same water is used for cooking. The result of this is the prevalence of dangerous, and even deadly diseases; namely, cholera, typhus, and dysentery. The second reason is
35 that the rivers that provide people's daily water needs

are often polluted. The source of the pollution is factories that use water along with toxic chemicals in industrial applications. These factories may then return untreated, highly polluted water to the rivers.

Figures published by the World Health Organization suggest that two billion people lack access to clean water and that each year more than 1.4 million people die from water-related diseases. Many of the victims are children. It is a sad fact that more people die each year because of a lack of clean water than those dying as a result of armed conflict.

Conflict, however, is a likely outcome of water scarcity. Rivers flow naturally from the mountains to the sea and ignore national boundaries. There are 286 major rivers in the world that cross national borders. As countries face diminishing supplies of water, they are likely to build dams to keep the water for their own consumption. China, for example, has dam projects that will affect India, Vietnam, and Laos.

Climate change is likely to accelerate water shortages in some areas of the world. Again, China provides an example. China's major rivers are fed from glaciers in the Himalayas and Tibetan plateau. Year by year, these glaciers are getting smaller. If they disappear, China's water supply will be further diminished, and China's ability to grow enough food to feed its population will suffer. Countries affected in such ways may see the emergence of protest movements among their populations.

It's time for people in the developed world to rethink their attitude toward water. It is evident that unrestricted development and using rivers as sewers is ridiculous. If we are to leave a habitable world for our grandchildren, we have to raise our consciousness about the way we treat water now.

C Understanding the text

Read the questions below and circle the correct answers according to the text.

1 **GIST** What is this text mainly about?
- **A** Polluted rivers
- **B** Access to clean water
- **C** Water problems

2 **MAIN IDEA** What is the main idea?
- **A** Access to sufficient and clean water will be increasingly limited in the future.
- **B** Climate change will cause serious water shortages in the future.
- **C** It is highly likely that water shortages will lead to political problems.

3 **DETAILS** International disputes over water supply are possible because …
- **A** people dump untreated waste into rivers.
- **B** climate change will cause glaciers to melt.
- **C** rivers flow through more than one country.

4 **DETAILS** Illnesses from polluted water kill …
- **A** more people than wars.
- **B** 3.4 million children each year.
- **C** people because of toxic industrial chemicals.

D Reference words

The words below are taken from the text. In each case, write down what they refer to.

1 *it*   (lines 1–3) _____

2 *this*   (line 6)   _____

3 *this*   (line 25)   _____

4 *those* (line 45)   _____

5 *they* (line 59)   _____

E Making inferences

Which two of these statements would the author of the text disagree with? Circle the correct answers. Then compare your answers with a partner.

1 As technology develops, water problems will diminish in the future.

2 In China, there may be protests as water supplies shrink.

3 Lack of sewer systems in developing countries leads to disease.

4 Climate change will result in more water for most countries.

5 China has lost water resources as a result of intense industrial and agricultural development.

Discuss it

Work with a partner or in a small group. Ask and answer the questions below.

1 Look back at the ideas you highlighted. Are they the same? What are the differences?

2 Some people suggest that technology such as making drinking water from seawater will solve water shortages. What do you think about this?

3 What are some ways that countries use water resources inefficiently?

Researching a topic

A Information gathering

The table below shows the total amount of water that comes into a country and how much water a country consumes in one year. Work with a partner. One is Student A; one is Student B. Student A: use the table below. Student B: use the table on page 98. Ask your partner for the missing information and complete the table.

Country	Total water resources per person per year (cubic meters)	Total consumption per person per year (cubic meters)
Canada		2,330
China	2,110	
Ireland		1,300
Israel	250	
Japan		1,380
Lebanon	1,070	2,110
Namibia	8,320	1,680
Portugal		2,510
Saudi Arabia	100	1,850
South Africa		1,260
South Korea	1,450	1,630
Spain	2,510	
Syria		2,110
UK	2,390	1,260
United Arab Emirates	30	
USA	9,850	2,840

Home Water Use

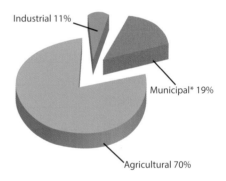

Showers and baths 35%
Toilet flushing 30%
Laundry 20%
Kitchen and drinking 10%
Cleaning 5%

Approximate figures for developed countries

Global Water Use

Industrial 11%
Municipal* 19%
Agricultural 70%

*includes home water use, urban landscaping, and irrigation

Source: Food and Agriculture Organization of the United Nations (FAO)

B Interpreting and reporting results

1 Work in small groups. Use the information in the table and graphs to discuss the questions below.

1 Which countries have the most water per person? What factors affect this amount?

2 Which countries consume the most water? Why do you think there are differences in consumption?

3 Some countries consume more than their resources. How might they do this?

4 The average Canadian uses about 343 liters of water per day in their home. This is just over 5 percent of their total water use. In what other ways is water used?

5 Other than exporting the water directly, what are some other ways to export water?

2 Share your group's ideas with the class.

One reason why some countries use more water than others could be ...

Apart from home use, water is also used in ...

One way a country can export water indirectly is by ...

5 Critical thinking

A Categorizing

Work with a partner. Look at the statements below that relate to how we use water. Match them to these categories. (There may be more than one correct answer.)

A Water across boundaries	**D** Water and technology	**F** Water demand
B Water and business	**E** Water conservation	**G** Water supply
C Water and pollution		

1 Minamata disease was caused by the dumping of mercury into the sea. _____

2 Intensive agriculture requires more water. _____

3 As glaciers disappear, some rivers will dry up. _____

4 People can adjust their daily habits so they use less water. _____

5 A dam in China may affect the availability of water in Vietnam. _____

6 Companies release industrial waste directly into rivers, and we all pay the costs of the cleanup. _____

7 Saudi Arabia converts seawater to drinking water. _____

8 The Aral Sea between Uzbekistan and Kazakhstan has lost 90 percent of its water because of irrigation projects in neighboring Russia. _____

9 A kilogram of beef protein requires approximately 10 times more water to produce than a kilo of soy protein. _____

B Diagramming

Choose one of the categories above and create a diagram as in the example below. Add boxes as necessary. You may want to refer back to the text on **page 20**.

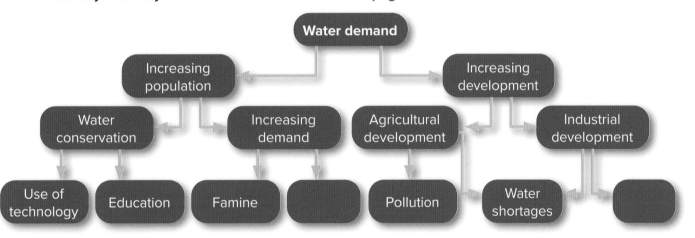

C Writing

The diagram has notes for two topic sentences:

1 An increasing population creates greater water demand.

2 Water demand becomes higher with increasing development.

Choose one topic sentence from your completed diagram and use the diagram to write a paragraph. An example is shown below.

> **topic sentence**
> a sentence that explains the main idea or ideas of a paragraph. It is often the first sentence of the paragraph.

An increasing population creates greater water demand. One result of this is the need for water conservation. There are at least two ways in which we can help conserve water. One is through the use of technology, while the other comes from education.

D Presentation

You are attending a world conference on water issues, where solutions are to be discussed. Below are some statements that people attending made before the conference. You are going to prepare a presentation at the conference that deals with one of these statements.

1 Work in small groups. Read the statements and choose one to discuss.

1 The supply of water should be limited during certain seasons.

2 Water is a human right. Countries with lots of water should give it free to others.

3 Countries with lots of water should export it to others.

4 Water should be much more expensive.

5 Dams that affect other countries shouldn't be built.

6 It's time to force countries to enter into agreements over water use.

7 Bottled water should be banned.

8 Governments should promote the benefits of tap water.

2 Prepare your presentation in your groups.

- List your reasons and arguments behind your statement.
- Think of details and examples to support your argument. Use the internet if you can.
- Consider both the advantages and disadvantages of your statement.

Introductions

> Today, we're going to discuss the topic of ...

> We'll start by looking at the main issues of ... We'll show that ...

> By the end, you will understand why we believe that ...

Conclusions

> So, to summarize the main points, today we have talked about ...

> Let's review the key points of the presentation. First ...

> To conclude, we hope we have shown you why we believe that ...

TIP

Structuring your presentation

A good presentation always consists of three basic parts: an introduction, body or middle section, and a conclusion. Create a general plan with these three parts before you think about the details.

- **Introduction**: this is where you welcome the audience and give them a "road map" for your talk.
- **Body**: this is the main part of your talk, where you make your points, explain your reasoning, and give examples to support your ideas.
- **Conclusion**: this is the final part, where you summarize your key points and main message and thank the audience for listening.

66 Quotable quotes
Final thoughts . . . 99

Globalization was supposed to break down barriers between continents and bring all peoples together. But what kind of globalization do we have with over one billion people on the planet not having safe water to drink?

Mikhail Gorbachev
Former Soviet leader

1 Why do you think Gorbachev connects safe drinking water with globalization?

2 How is this quote connected to the cartoon at the beginning of this unit?

3 Gorbachev suggests that access to safe drinking water is a human right. Do you agree?

Fished Out: Our Empty Oceans

CHRIS MADDEN.

In this unit, you will:

- read an article about overfishing in the Atlantic.
- read an article about the effects of global overfishing.
- discuss the issue of commercial fishing limits.

1 Critical cartoons

A Building knowledge

Work with a partner or in a small group. Look at the information on this page and the cartoon. Discuss the questions below.

1 What are some kinds of fish that are being overfished?

2 Do you avoid any marine food products because they are being overfished?

3 What are some of the effects of overfishing?

4 What is the message of the cartoon? What is the connection to the unit topic?

> I heard that ... are being overfished.

> I try not to eat ... because ...

> Overfishing can lead to ...

> Maybe this cartoon is trying to show that ...

MEDIA link

Seaspiracy (2021) is a documentary film by British filmmaker Ali Tabrizi about the impact of fishing on the environment and on marine life. It calls for the end of fish consumption.

For additional media links, go to infocus-eltseries.com

2 Core vocabulary

A Skimming and scanning

1 Find and underline the keywords in the text. Try to guess their meanings.

Keywords

ancestor	biodiversity	biologist	continent	degrade
rational	shallow	stabilize	treaty	widespread

The Grand Banks

There is no greater example of the dangers of overfishing than the Grand Banks of Newfoundland. Banks are large shallow areas in the seas next to the coasts of continents. One feature of the Grand Banks is the temperature of the water, which is the result of the Gulf Stream bringing warm water from the Gulf of Mexico to the Banks. The shallow depth and mixing of the warm Gulf Stream with the cold Labrador Current create conditions that allow a biodiversity of animal life.
5 The banks once supported large populations of fish, especially cod, and other sea creatures.

In the 1500s, knowledge of the Banks became widespread, and many countries began to send fishing fleets to the area. The ancestors of European and North American fishermen used small wooden boats and didn't catch many fish, so the cod population remained stable. Later, more efficient fishing boats, known as trawlers, were designed. These pulled a large net called a trawl. With the invention of steam and diesel engines in the 1870s, trawlers became more powerful,
10 and the nets they pulled became bigger. They dragged their nets over the bottom of the sea, catching many kinds of unwanted fish in their nets. There was a lot of waste, and the action of the nets degraded the local environment. People simply turned a blind eye to this situation. Eventually, biologists who were studying the cod population began to warn of future problems. They argued that the rational outcome of continuing in this way would be the collapse of the cod fisheries. In this case, the word "collapse" has a special meaning: it means that the population falls to less than 10 percent
15 of the original population. Other experts claimed that the Grand Banks were too large for humans to affect. However, over time, the catches became smaller. Populations of fish couldn't stabilize as the gap between the harvest and the replacement rate continued to expand.

In 1977, Canada began to regulate fishing in a 320-kilometer zone based on an international treaty, partly to protect the declining fish stock. However, other countries continued to overfish, and in the early 1990s, the cod population finally
20 collapsed. In 1992, to prevent the Atlantic cod from becoming extinct, the Canadian government stopped all cod fishing. More than 30 years later, the cod population in the area has still not recovered.

2 Look at the pictures below. Which picture goes best with the text above? Circle A, B, or C. Then explain your answer to a partner.

A

B

C

B Words in context: register

synonym
a word or phrase that has the same or nearly the same meaning as another word or phrase

1 "Register" refers to the degree of formality in language. Match the keyword in each sentence below from the text to its least formal synonym.

   1 There was a lot of waste, and the action of the nets **degraded** the local environment.

      A sullied
      B despoiled
      C damaged

   2 They argued that the **rational** outcome of continuing in this way would be the collapse of the cod fisheries.

      A coherent
      B logical
      C plausible

   3 In the 1500s, knowledge of the Banks became **widespread**, and many countries began to send fishing fleets to the area.

      A well known
      B prevalent
      C pervasive

2 Now rewrite in your own words each of the sentences above using the least formal synonym. Where possible, match the tone of the sentence to the synonym.

   1 _____

   2 _____

   3 _____

C Vocabulary building: idioms　Example: *turn a blind eye*

idiom
a group of words that together have a meaning that is different from the meanings of the separate words

1 Below are some idioms with the word *turn*. Match each idiom to its meaning.

turn a blind eye	to imagine or remember times in the past
turn over a new leaf	to decide not to do anything to hurt a person who has hurt you
turn the other cheek	to ignore something that you know is wrong
turn back the clock	to change your behavior in a positive way

2 Complete the sentences below with the correct idiom. Change the word forms as necessary.

   1 Let's _____ and play some music from the 70s.

   2 Mika was upset when her best friend shouted at her, but she _____.

   3 The limited resources forced the police to _____ to the problem.

   4 The doctor's warning motivated Achara to _____ and take up jogging.

3 Now use the idioms to make your own sentences.

D Discussion dictation

1 Listen and write down the questions. Then discuss them in small groups.

   1 _____ ?

   2 _____ ?

   3 _____ ?

2 Form new groups and compare your answers.

3 Reading skills

A Pre-reading

1 Quickly scan the text and circle the 10 keywords.

2 How are the fish-eating habits of people in developing countries changing?

3 Fish is an important part of a healthy diet. Are there any problems that come from people eating more fish? If so, what are they?

B Reading

Read the text and check your answers to the pre-reading questions above. Then highlight an interesting idea in each paragraph.

Our Desert Oceans

Our ancestors hunted many types of wild animals. Today, the only wild animals hunted in significant numbers are fish. The numbers truly are significant: many fish species that used to be widespread are
5 now threatened with extinction.

In the sixteenth century, when Europeans first sailed across the Atlantic to the northeast coast of the North American continent, they were amazed at the abundance of fish in the shallow waters of the
10 Grand Banks. Stories at the time describe how it was possible to catch fish from the sea using a basket. The promise of a rich fishing industry along with the fur trade provided the economic basis for early exploration of that part
15 of the world. For the next 300 years, fishing was the backbone of the area's economy. Today, though, the fish
20 are largely gone. In the early 1990s, the fishing industry in Newfoundland collapsed, and despite efforts to help fish stocks
25 to recover, they haven't done so. Some marine biologists suggest that the ecosystem has changed and that it might
30 not be possible to return the environment to what it was before and stabilize it at previous levels.

According to the World Wildlife Fund, the capacity of the world's fishing fleets is two to three times what is sustainable over the long term. However, it isn't just
35 the number of fishing boats that is the problem: fishing technology has changed enormously over the last 30 years. A technique called bottom trawling allows for very large nets to be dragged across the ocean floor. Giant rubber rollers prevent the nets from getting
40 caught and breaking on rocks and coral. These rollers also destroy coral and other fish habitats. The result is a desert on the ocean floor where nothing can live.

Modern fishing methods like these result in everything being caught, not just the fish species targeted. These unlucky fish and other marine animals, known as "bycatch," are often thrown back dead into the sea. They may not have commercial value, but they are essential to the marine ecosystem. Other destructive fishing methods include cyanide fishing, where fish are poisoned to make them easier to catch, and dynamite fishing, where fish are killed by underwater explosions. Both these methods degrade and sometimes destroy the marine environment.

This unsustainable rush to grab as much of the world's marine resources as possible before they disappear is a modern tragedy. It is driven by self-interest and an increasing desire to consume fish, especially among developing nations. As the wealth of a country increases, so does protein consumption by its population.

Attempts to regulate fishing in a rational way face many problems. First, there is the fact that much of the ocean is outside the territory of a single nation. Any rules must therefore be negotiated through international treaties. Some countries with large fishing fleets don't support regulation. They may even provide subsidies to the fishing industry. In fact, 20 percent of global fishing revenues comes from government subsidies. The second problem relates to enforcement. The oceans are vast and resources are limited. Pirate fishing boats are motivated by huge profits, and the chance of being caught is low.

We have no clear idea of the final result of our overfishing. In some respects, we know more about the moon than we do about the ocean. But one thing is certain: unless we do something about this massive attack upon our ocean environment and its biodiversity, we may be the last generation to know what it is like to eat wild fish.

C Understanding the text

Read the questions below and circle the correct answers according to the text.

1 GIST What is this text mainly about?

   A Overfishing
   B Pollution in the ocean
   C The importance of eating fish

2 MAIN IDEA What is the main idea?

   A Fishing technology has improved a lot in the last 30 years.
   B We need to limit and control fishing before it is too late.
   C Countries are beginning to cooperate to save our oceans.

3 DETAILS The capacity of the global fishing fleet has increased because ...

   A there are many more fishing boats.
   B fishing technology has improved.
   C of both the above reasons.

4 DETAILS Regulating fishing is difficult because ...

   A the oceans cover a very large area.
   B the fish are getting harder to catch.
   C people enjoy eating fish.

D Reference words

The words below are taken from the text. In each case, write down what they refer to.

1 *they* (line 8) _____

2 *they* (line 25) _____

3 *what* (line 33) _____

4 *These unlucky fish* (lines 44–45) _____

5 *It* (line 55) _____

E Making inferences

Which two of the following statements would the author probably disagree with? Circle the correct answers. Then compare your answers with a partner.

1 The oceans of the world are so large that fishing has only a local impact.

2 If one fish species becomes endangered, we can't simply choose a different species to fish.

3 Fishing regulations are often ignored.

4 Government fishing subsidies are a major problem.

5 Fish farming is the answer to the overfishing problem.

Discuss it

Work with a partner or in a small group. Ask and answer the questions below.

1 Look back at the ideas you highlighted. Are they the same? What are the differences?

2 Overfishing is similar to climate change: no single nation can find a solution. Do you agree? Why or why not?

3 Fish farming is sometimes suggested as a solution to overfishing. What do you think?

4 The author suggests that we know more about the moon than the ocean. Why do you think this is?

4 Researching a topic

A Information gathering

Study the information about five commonly eaten fish. Work with a partner. One is Student A; one is Student B. Student A: use the table below. Student B: use the table on **page 98**. Ask your partner for the missing information and complete your table.

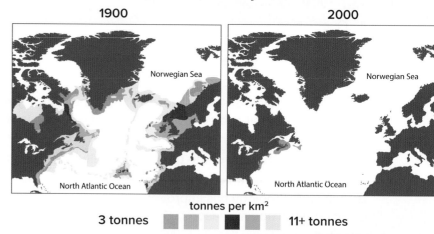

Catch of commonly eaten fish

1900   2000

Norwegian Sea

North Atlantic Ocean

tonnes per km²

3 tonnes   11+ tonnes

Fish facts					
Species	Atlantic cod	Atlantic halibut	Haddock	Sole	Bluefin tuna
Comments	Less than 10% of maximum stock levels	Reaches maturity at 10 years old; can live to be over 50			Population down nearly 90 percent since 1970s
FAO status*		Depleted	Depleted		Depleted
Tonnes of fish caught per year (1,000)					
1950	2,080	22		369	
2000		4	213		83
2010	952		396	433	

Source: Food and Agriculture Organization of the United Nations (FAO)
*FAO status: under-exploited, moderately exploited, fully exploited, over-exploited, depleted (= shrinking population)

B Interpreting and reporting results

1 Work in small groups. Discuss the questions below.

1 What information do the maps tell us? Describe the changes.

2 What is the situation for each of the fish since 1950? Briefly summarize the changes.

3 According to the data, what is the latest situation for each fish? Which fish stock has decreased most since 1950?

4 The FAO designates some wild fish species as depleted, yet the catches have not always decreased. Can you explain this?

2 Share your group's ideas with the class.

Since 1950, stocks of ... have gone from ... to ...

The most rapid/largest decrease has been ...

According to the FAO, the current status of ... is ...

We can see there has been a big decline in ...

5 Critical thinking

A Fact or opinion?

Two people are discussing a possible new United Nations law of the sea that would limit the number of fish caught. Jan Helberg is president of a canned-fish company. Linda Wong teaches marine biology to graduate students and works as a volunteer consultant to the World Wildlife Fund.

Work with a partner. Decide who made the following statements and whether they are facts (F) or opinions (O).

Statement	Who said	Fact or opinion
1 "Many fish stocks are healthy. A new law is not needed."		
2 "People have fished for thousands of years; the fish industry is just more efficient now."		
3 "We need regulation now. Many fish stocks are already depleted."		
4 "We need to do more research before signing the treaty."		
5 "Jobs may be lost in the short term but saved in the long term."		

B Understanding reasoning

In Unit 2, we introduced four types of reasoning used in discussions: cause and effect, conditional, comparative, and pros and cons. Another type of reasoning is analogical. This is when we compare two things that are similar and use them to predict other similarities.

Jan and Linda are discussing the new law. What types of reasoning do they use? Identify the types and underline the words that support your answers. Compare your answers with a partner.

Type of reasoning

Linda: If we save the fish, there will be jobs for people in the future.   _____

Jan: The treaty may save a few fish. On the other hand, it will destroy our economy and put 100,000 people out of work.   _____

Linda: Commercial fishing is like mass murder. It can't be justified.   _____

Jan: But countries that have signed the treaty have smaller fishing fleets than others. Some of them have no coastline!   _____

Linda: Signing the treaty today will mean our grandchildren can eat fish.   _____

C Writing

Look at the statements in A and B above. Write a paragraph that describes your opinion about commercial fishing. Try to use all five of the types of reasoning. Then compare your paragraph with a partner. An example is shown below.

In my opinion, we need to ban commercial fishing completely in some areas. The first reason is to protect commercial fishing in the long term. If we don't create a ban, commercial fishing will be gone forever. The threat is like ...

D Role play and debate

Should our country sign the treaty limiting commercial fishing?

You are going to take part in a TV debate on whether your country should sign the treaty limiting commercial fishing. The panel consists of these people.

Sergio Martinez is a 47-year-old Spanish deep-sea fisherman. If Spain signs the treaty, he will be out of work. He is married with four children. His oldest daughter is about to enter college.	**Wendy Smith,** 52, owns a small fish restaurant in Monterey, California. She is afraid that if the United States signs the treaty, the cost of fish will drive away customers. She has no pension.	**Manzo Nagano** is a 68-year-old Japanese environmentalist, and he is lobbying for Japan to sign the treaty. He used to teach marine biology at a major university.	**Ali Dembry** is a 21-year-old arts student at a private college in Sydney. She is a strict vegan. Ali opposes all fishing and believes that aggressive and direct action is necessary.

1 Work in small groups, (4 people, if possible). Your teacher will ask you to be one of the characters. Debate the issues in your groups. Before you begin, think about your character and prepare your arguments carefully. Refer to the information in this unit as necessary.

- Support your argument with examples.
- Refer to common sense.
- Use examples, statistics, and expert opinion.

> According to world experts, ...

> A good example of this can be seen ...

> If you look at the latest statistics on ... we can see that ...

> As the expert ... states ...

TIP

Voicing your opinion

There are three parts to giving your opinion in a discussion or debate:

1 State your opinion.

2 Give a reason for your opinion.

3 Provide some evidence: examples, statistics, and expert opinion.

You can use many expressions to state your opinion and explain your reasoning. The expressions here help you provide evidence.

2 Share your ideas with the class. Take a vote. Do most classmates vote to sign the treaty?

Quotable quotes
Final thoughts . . .

The sea, the great unifier, is man's only hope. Now, as never before, the old phrase has a literal meaning: we are all in the same boat.

Jacques Yves Cousteau
French oceanographer and co-inventor of the SCUBA tank

1 Apart from overfishing, in what other ways do humans damage the oceans? Which are most serious?

2 What does Cousteau mean by "we are all in the same boat"?

3 What are some actions that people can take to help the oceans?

In this unit, you will:

- read an article about green energy.
- read an article about nuclear power.
- discuss different points of view regarding energy sources.

1 Critical cartoons

A Building knowledge

Work with a partner or in a small group. Look at the information on this page and the cartoon. Discuss the questions below.

1 What are the main ways energy is created for our daily needs?

2 What is your image of green energy, like wind or solar energy? How about nuclear energy?

3 Do you know of any problems or disadvantages of green energy? What are they?

4 What is the message of the cartoon? What is the connection to the unit topic?

> I think most of our energy is created from ...

> My image of nuclear energy is ...

> One problem with wind energy is ...

> I think the point of the cartoon is to ...

MEDIA link

Nuclear Now (2022) is a documentary by American director Oliver Stone. It makes a strong case that nuclear energy is a necessary and obvious solution to climate change.

For additional media links, go to infocus-eltseries.com

A Skimming and scanning

1 Find and underline the keywords in the text. Try to guess their meanings.

Keywords

accumulation	consensus	contrary	controversy	empirical
impact	neutral	rejection	statistically	transmission

Green Energy?

How does an environmentalist become a supporter of nuclear energy? Consider the disasters at Three Mile Island, Chornobyl, and Fukushima. They seem to cry out for the rejection of nuclear power. The impact of these nuclear accidents has made many people afraid of nuclear power. This has led many greens to reject nuclear energy. However, not all greens are convinced that nuclear energy is bad. For one such green, Gwyneth Cravens, the journey began with global
5 warming theory. Almost all scientists have now reached a consensus that the earth is warming. They believe that the use of fuels such as coal and oil are the main reasons for the warming. For greens, the controversy is not global warming, but what should be done about it. Most green organizations support the use of clean energy sources, such as wind or solar power.

For Cravens, nuclear power should also be considered green energy. At first, she was against nuclear power and
10 protested against it. Then, she met an expert in nuclear risk assessment. He urged her to take a neutral position and to give up her opposition to nuclear energy. He explained that modern society needs a continuous transmission of electricity, 24 hours a day, seven days a week. He pointed out that power sources like wind and solar energy could not be relied upon for this. Only nuclear, coal, or hydropower sources can do this. He invited her to go on a tour of a nuclear power station in the United States. She looked at the empirical data, such as the amount of CO_2 given off and the volume
15 of waste created in production. She found that waste from coal also contained statistically significant quantities of radioactive materials. For Cravens, the accumulation of evidence led her to conclude that nuclear energy is necessary. So, after nearly 10 years of studying the issues, she took the position contrary to her original one and began to support nuclear energy.

2 Look at the pictures below. Which picture goes best with the text above? Circle A, B, or C. Then explain your answer to a partner.

A

B

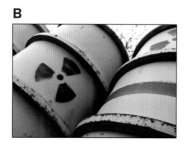

C

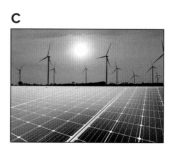

B Words in context: definitions

1 Look at the definitions of the three keywords below. Find the definition that matches how each word is used in the text on **page 34**.

impact
1 the force or action of one object hitting another
2 the effect that a person, event, or situation has on someone or something
3 to affect something or someone

rejection
1 refusing to accept or agree with someone or something
2 letter or document that says you have not been successful in getting a job, a place at college, etc.
3 not giving someone else the love or attention they were expecting

transmission
1 the process of broadcasting something by radio, television, etc., or something that is broadcast
2 the system in a car that moves power from its engine to its wheels
3 the process of passing something from one person or place to another

2 Make your own sentences using the keywords and compare them with a partner. Which meanings does your partner use?

1 _____

2 _____

3 _____

C Vocabulary building: word parts: *trans*   Example: *transmission*

Words with *trans*

| transatlantic | transfer | translate | translucent | transport |

1 Use the words in the box to complete the sentences below. Change the word form as necessary. Try to guess the meaning of any words you don't know.

1 Frankfurt is a major _____ hub in Germany.

2 Mila _____ to a university in California.

3 My grandparents sailed to New York on a _____ liner.

4 Professor Shadbolt _____ six Russian poems.

5 The curtains were _____—letting light in but protecting privacy.

2 Work with a partner. What do you think *trans* means? Write your guess below. Then check your answer with another partner.

I think *trans* means _____.

D Discussion dictation

1 Listen and write down the questions. Then discuss them in small groups.

1 _____ ?

2 _____ ?

3 _____ ?

2 Form new groups and compare your answers.

A Pre-reading

1 Quickly scan the text and circle the 10 keywords.

2 Which is safer, nuclear power or solar power?

3 How many people in the United States have died as a result of nuclear power use?

A 0   **B** 20   **C** 200   **D** 2,000

B Reading

Read the text and check your answers to the pre-reading questions above. Then highlight an interesting idea in each paragraph.

The ONE Energy Solution

When monitoring of atmospheric CO_2 began in 1957, its concentration stood at 315 parts per million by volume. Before the Industrial Revolution, it is estimated that the atmospheric CO_2 concentration
5 was 280. In May of 2022, it reached 421. There is now a strong consensus among climate scientists that increased concentrations of CO_2 in the atmosphere cause warming both on land and in the ocean. There is also a consensus that this warming will lead to
10 serious environmental problems, such as rising sea levels and extreme weather events.

The use of fossil fuels, namely coal and oil, is responsible for this increase in CO_2. At the present rate of fossil fuel use, the impact of heat energy that
15 we are putting into the atmosphere and oceans is equivalent to at least four Hiroshima-sized atomic bombs every second. This can't continue. Even if we completely stopped burning fossil fuels today, warming would continue because of the CO_2 already
20 in the atmosphere. If this warming continues at the present rate, average temperatures by 2040 are likely to rise on average by 1.5 degrees Celsius above pre-industrial levels. This will have serious negative environmental and economic effects globally.

25 Something has to be done to minimize the CO_2 we release. We could try to drastically cut back on our energy use, but this is both impractical—it would require a massive drop in our standard of living—and is also contrary to ideas of fairness. How can we tell
30 developing countries, which aspire to developed countries' standard of living, to stop developing?

Renewable
35 energy is clean, but, unfortunately, renewable energy sources such as wind and solar power are
40 unable to satisfy our energy needs. Wind and geothermal energy

hold promise but are limited to particular locations. Solar energy is also restricted to certain areas: in high northern and southern latitudes, for example, the sunlight is much weaker. Solar and wind power also have a major limitation in that they can't guarantee a steady transmission of energy: both depend on the weather. And solar power, of course, provides no energy at night. Energy storage is therefore essential. Using batteries or pumping water to a higher elevation and then using this water to drive a turbine are two storage methods, but they result in quite large losses of efficiency.

This leads to one solution. The only non-CO_2-producing energy source that will provide sufficient energy at a reasonable cost is nuclear. Nuclear power provides the only practical alternative to fossil fuels. Accidents at Chornobyl and more recently Fukushima have created controversy and, in some cases, rejection of nuclear power. However, in Western countries, not one person has died as a result of a nuclear accident so far. Statistically, nuclear power is safer than solar power: solar panel installers sometimes fall off roofs. Opponents of nuclear power bring up the question of the accumulation of radioactive waste products, but in modern, efficient reactors, these can be recycled, actually producing more power. Opponents also fear that nuclear material will get into the hands of terrorists, but this risk can be eliminated with adequate security.

Climate change is real and serious, and its effects are just beginning to be felt around the world in the form of severe weather events. Minimizing its effects will require drastically reducing our reliance on fossil fuels. If we look at the empirical evidence in a neutral, objective way, it is clear that the use of nuclear power is key to avoiding a disastrous future.

C Understanding the text

Read the questions below and circle the correct answers according to the text.

1 **GIST** What is this text mainly about?
   A The best way to avoid climate change
   B Climate change problems
   C The need for nuclear power

2 **MAIN IDEA** The safest and most practical energy source for the world is …
   A nuclear.
   B solar.
   C geothermal.

3 **DETAILS** Wind power is not practical everywhere because …
   A wind turbines can't be located everywhere.
   B wind turbines are too expensive.
   C wind doesn't have enough energy.

4 **DETAILS** Even if we stop using fossil fuels, global warming will continue because …
   A of the CO_2 that remains in the atmosphere.
   B of other energy sources that also cause warming.
   C of negative environmental effects.

D Recognizing contrasts

1 In the text, five sentences describe contrasts using the word *but*. Find the sentences and complete each one in your own words.

   1 (Lines 26–27) *We could try to drastically cut back on our energy use …*
   2 (Lines 34–35) *Renewable energy is clean …*
   3 (Lines 41–43) *Wind and geothermal energy hold promise …*
   4 (Lines 63–65) *Opponents of nuclear power bring up the question of the accumulation of radioactive waste products …*
   5 (Lines 67–68) *Opponents also fear that nuclear material will get into the hands of terrorists …*

2 Compare your answers with a partner.

E Making inferences

Which one of the statements below can be inferred from the text? Circle the correct answer. Then compare your answers with a partner.

1 Solar power isn't practical in the far north or south because it is too cold.
2 Solar power would be more attractive if energy storage was more efficient.
3 Nuclear power plants have sufficient security.

Work with a partner or in a small group. Ask and answer the questions below.

1 Look back at the ideas you highlighted. Are they the same? What are the differences?

2 In what ways does your lifestyle contribute to energy consumption? What specific things would you be willing to do to reduce it?

3 Would you work in a nuclear power plant if you were offered a very high salary? Why or why not?

4 Researching a topic

A Information gathering

The two biggest nuclear accidents to date happened in Chornobyl, Ukraine, and Fukushima, Japan. Work with a partner. One is Student A; one is Student B. Student A: use the table below. Student B: use the table on **page 99**. Ask your partner for the missing information and complete the table.

Chornobyl and Fukushima Nuclear Accidents	Chornobyl	Fukushima
Number of deaths	64	
Number of years plant was in operation before accident	9	
Amount of nuclear fuel in plant (tonnes)	180	
Number of people relocated	335,000	
Highest level of radiation detected (mSv/hour)	200,000	

Notes
- The radiation limit for nuclear power workers in the United States is 50 mSv/year.
- Approximately 50 percent of people exposed to 4,000 to 5,000 mSv over a short period will die within one month.
- The wind in Japan was blowing from west to east at the time of the accident. This was normal for the time of the year.

B Interpreting and reporting results

1 Work in small groups. Discuss the questions below.

   1 Compare the two accidents. What is similar and what is different about them?

   2 Look at the highest radiation figures and information about radiation limits. What does this tell you about the danger of these accidents?

   3 What effect did the wind in Japan have on the scale of the accident? What if the wind had blown from the other direction or the accident had happened at Kashiwazaki-Kariwa?

2 Share your group's ideas with the class.

> What stands out to us is the fact that ...

> If you look at the figures, it's clear that ...

> In our group, we noticed the following similarities/differences: first ...

5 Critical thinking

A Fact or opinion?

William Whitfield is a 22-year-old graduate student in the English Literature department. For the past month, he has been protesting outside a nuclear plant. Dr. Roxanne Parker, 52 years old, is a nuclear physicist and director of safety and security at the plant.

1 Read the statements below. Who said what? Check (✓) the boxes. Then decide if the statements are fact (F) or opinion (O).

Statement	Whitfield	Parker	Fact or opinion
1 "Nuclear power can never be safe."			
2 "The plant has never had an accident since its construction 40 years ago."			
3 "Nuclear power is the only realistic energy option for the future."			
4 "No amount of exposure to radiation is safe."			
5 "Radiation is a natural part of the environment and surrounds us all the time."			

2 Work in small groups and compare your answers. Explain your choices.

> We think it's likely/unlikely that Dr. Parker said ... because ...

> I don't agree with the statement ... because ...

B Diagramming

Work in small groups. On the right is part of a diagram showing the pros and cons of nuclear power. Add your own ideas to the map. Add boxes as necessary. You may want to refer back to the texts on **pages 34** and **36**.

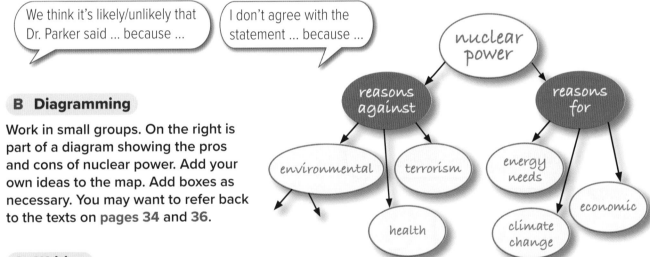

C Writing

Use the information in your diagram to write a paragraph that describes your opinion. The phrases and expressions below may help you.

There are many issues to consider on the topic of nuclear power.

One area of concern is ...

Another is ...

Some people argue that ...

Others state ...

After considering the arguments, my personal opinion is ...

D Role play and debate

The four members of a government council described below are drafting a policy about the country's future energy needs. In five years' time, current energy supplies will no longer be enough. In 10 years' time, the shortage of energy will cause severe economic problems for the country.

Miguel: a 30-year-old union worker who favors building a nuclear power plant. He is interested in the jobs it will create. He has three young children.

Emilia: a 25-year-old environmentalist. Emilia favors wind and solar power and slow economic growth. She is a single mother with one young child.

Bob: a 65-year-old car factory executive. He favors coal because it is the cheapest energy. He has two grown children.

Ye-Jin: a 60-year-old retired teacher who favors energy conservation and a decrease in economic activity. She has no children.

1 Work in small groups. Read the statements. Who do you think said what?

   1 "If we reduce our level of consumption and switch to renewables, we won't need new nuclear plants."

   2 "Environmentalists care more about trees and birds than they do about working men and their families."

   3 "In my business, cost is the bottom line. Nuclear power is just too expensive."

   4 "Nuclear power is a ticking time bomb. Think of our children's future."

2 In your groups, choose one of the four characters. What are other statements your character might make to support their opinion? Write three more statements below.

   Your group's character: _____

   1 _____

   2 _____

   3 _____

3 Form new groups of three or four people. Each group member should represent a different character. Use the statements you wrote and debate the issues.

4 Share your results with the class. Which council member's advice is most popular?

> I see what you're saying, but what about ...?

> I don't think you've thought about ...

> That's a good point.

> I couldn't agree with you more!

66 Quotable quotes
Final thoughts . . . 99

We want to end the use of nuclear energy and reach the age of renewable energy as fast as possible.

Angela Merkel
Former German chancellor

RADIOACTIVE WASTE

1 Merkel made this comment right after the Fukushima disaster. As a consequence, Germany became dependent on fossil fuel imports from other countries. Was Merkel's decision a good one?

2 How might world politics be different if we were not dependent on oil and gas imports from certain countries for our energy?

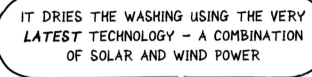

IT DRIES THE WASHING USING THE VERY *LATEST* TECHNOLOGY – A COMBINATION OF SOLAR AND WIND POWER

In this unit, you will:

- read an article about wind energy.
- read an article about different types of renewable energy.
- discuss and present on the pros and cons of renewable energy sources.

1 Critical cartoons

A Building knowledge

Work with a partner or in a small group. Look at the information on this page and the cartoon. Discuss the questions below.

1 How many sources of energy can you name? List them.

2 Which sources do you think are the cleanest? Which are the most efficient? Why?

3 What are some ways a country or people can save energy?

4 Why is the cartoon humorous? What is the connection to the unit topic?

... is an important source of energy.

I think ... energy is pretty clean.

A good way to save energy is ...

This cartoon made me smile because ...

MEDIA link

2040 (2019) is a documentary by award-winning Australian director Damon Gameau. Concerned about his daughter's future, Gameau travels the world in search of new and better solutions to deal with the problems of climate change.

For additional media links, go to infocus-eltseries.com

A Skimming and scanning

1 Find and underline the keywords in the text. Try to guess their meanings.

Keywords

bulk	exploit	finite	infinite	likewise
obtain	reliability	solar	transformation	utilize

Winds of Change

The northern European country of Denmark used to produce so much oil that it exported it to other countries. Its oil and natural gas resources were mostly found in the North Sea. The country used oil for many things other than powering cars—10 years ago, the bulk of Denmark's electricity was produced using oil. However, the Danish government realized that oil was a finite energy source that would run out someday. It accepted the need to obtain a different source of

5　energy, ideally one that seemed infinite. The government also knew that the energy source had to meet certain criteria. The energy had to be reliable and able to be produced every day, despite varying conditions. Solar panels have problems with reliability because they produce electricity only when the sun shines. Likewise, land windmills suffer from reliability problems: very often, the wind is not strong enough. However, off the coast of Denmark, the wind blows constantly, and furthermore, the sea is only 5 to 15 meters deep. The Danish government decided this was an excellent natural resource

10　to exploit, and it encouraged the construction of windmills up and down the coast. As a result, wind power now produces 57 percent of all the electricity used in the country.

Denmark's transformation from oil exploiter to green power leader continues today. In 2012, the government launched a plan to produce 50 percent of its electricity from wind by 2020. It has now achieved this goal. Danish companies have gained more than government contracts to build the windmills. They have utilized their knowledge to good advantage

15　and now stand as world leaders in wind power.

2　**Read the statements below. Which best summarizes the text? Circle A, B, or C. Then explain your answer to a partner.**

　A Denmark has moved from oil-based energy to wind power.

　B Denmark needs a reliable energy source.

　C There are various reasons why solar energy isn't suitable in Denmark.

B Words in context: register

1 "Register" refers to the degree of formality in language. Match the keyword in each sentence below from the text to its least formal synonym.

1 It accepted the need to **obtain** a different source of energy.

    A secure
    B find
    C acquire

2 Denmark's **transformation** from oil exploiter to green power continues today.

    A change
    B conversion
    C adjustment

3 They have **utilized** their knowledge to good advantage and now stand as world leaders in wind power.

    A develop
    B exploited
    C used

2 Now rewrite in your own words each of the sentences above using the least formal synonym. Where possible, match the tone of the sentence to the synonym.

1 _____

2 _____

3 _____

C Vocabulary building: phrasal verbs   Example: *run out (of)*

Phrasal verbs with *run*

run across	run out of	run through	run up against

1 Read the sentence in the text with the phrasal verb *run out* (line 4) and the sentences below. Guess the meaning of each phrasal verb. Then compare them with a partner.

1 Let's run through our strategy once more to make sure we've thought of everything.

2 The IT department ran up against all kinds of problems trying to introduce the new technology.

3 When I was tidying up my bedroom, I ran across an old photo.

2 Use the phrasal verbs in the box to complete the sentences below. Change the word form as necessary.

1 After waiting to be rescued for over three days, the flood victims were beginning to _____ hope.

2 In all our years in business, we have never _____ a tougher competitor.

3 Lena _____ several friends when she visited her hometown.

4 Make sure you begin by _____ the key points when you present at the meeting.

3 Use the phrasal verbs to make your own sentences. Then compare them with a partner.

D Discussion dictation

1 Listen and write down the questions. Then discuss them in small groups.

1 _____ ?

2 _____ ?

3 _____ ?

2 Form new groups and compare your answers.

3 Reading skills

A Pre-reading

1 Quickly scan the text and circle the 10 keywords.

2 What are two advantages of nuclear power?

3 What are three ways of using the sun's energy?

B Reading

Read the text and check your answers to the pre-reading questions above. Then highlight an interesting idea in each paragraph.

Beyond Fossil Fuels

For the bulk of human history, people used renewable energy. They burned plant material, usually wood, to create fires for light, warmth, and cooking. Following the birth of agriculture 10,000 years ago, animal and
5 human muscle power was used to plow fields, carry heavy loads, and pull up water from wells. It was much later, after the Industrial Revolution, when people began to exploit non-renewable fossil fuels, such as coal, oil, and gas. These concentrated energy sources
10 made the creation of modern civilization possible, and today we have become energy addicts, consuming more and more as the world develops. However, this can't continue. People may debate how much oil and coal is left under the ground or sea, but one thing is
15 certain: the supply of fossil fuels is finite. We may not know when this energy source will run out, but one day it will, and the impact is likely to be terrible.

We need a transformation in the way we obtain and use energy. But how are we to do it? Some suggest
20 we should turn to nuclear energy as a virtually inexhaustible energy source. They claim that nuclear energy is clean and produces no greenhouse gases. This might be true, but the risk of an accident like in Chornobyl or Fukushima, or the spread of nuclear
25 materials to a terrorist organization or state, makes our reliance on nuclear power unacceptable. We are left with renewable energy sources. Not wood this time, but biofuel and wind, solar, geothermal, and hydroelectric power. Geothermal and hydroelectric
30 power, while important, exist only in a limited number of regions. So this leaves biofuel and wind and solar power to provide us with the energy needs of the future.

Wind power is not new. Since long ago, we have
35 utilized the power of the wind to sail across the oceans, and many are familiar with windmills used to grind corn or draw water from wells. In the past 40 years or so, advances in technology have enabled wind-powered generation of electricity to become an economic reality. Denmark has become the world leader in this regard, and 57 percent of its electricity now comes from giant wind turbines. Denmark even sells electricity to neighboring countries. The country plans to be completely free of fossil fuels by 2050.

Solar power also has great potential. In a single year, we receive twice as much energy from the sun as that contained in all the earth's remaining non-renewable resources, such as coal, oil, natural gas, and uranium. For practical purposes, the sun's energy is infinite. We can capture some of this energy by designing smart buildings; for example, ones in the northern hemisphere with most windows facing south and few facing north. This is known as passive solar power. Another way is to use the sun's energy to convert water to steam and have this steam drive an electric generator. A third way is to use a solar cell to produce electricity directly. Solar power holds great promise, but its reliability in the far north and south is questionable.

Biofuel is made by fermenting plant material, such as corn or sugarcane, to generate ethanol. This ethanol can then be used directly as a fuel or mixed with gasoline. Biodiesel is made from plant or animal fats and usually added to diesel fuel. Unfortunately, experts point out that biofuel isn't as environmentally friendly as other renewable energy sources because it produces CO_2 when burned. Likewise, critics complain that it takes away land that could be used to grow food.

The costs of some renewable energy technologies, such as solar and wind, have dropped significantly over the past decade. In many regions, they have become competitive with or even cheaper than new coal or gas-fired power plants. It is clear that the path to a future environmentally friendly world, one with sufficient energy for all, lies in our investment in renewable energy today and its use tomorrow.

C Understanding the text

Read the questions below and circle the correct answers according to the text.

1 **GIST** What is this text mainly about?

    A Greenhouse gases

    B Future energy sources

    C The danger of nuclear power

2 **MAIN IDEA** What is the main idea?

    A There are advantages and disadvantages of renewable energy sources.

    B Non-renewable energy sources are important but can be dangerous.

    C We need to shift to renewable energy sources like wind power.

3 **DETAILS** The author identifies two problems with nuclear power. What are they?

    A Nuclear accidents, if they occur, are very dangerous.

    B Terrorists might obtain nuclear material.

    C Nuclear power is very expensive.

4 **DETAILS** Which two of the following statements are true?

    A Denmark currently gets about a quarter of its electric power from wind.

    B Denmark is an energy exporter.

    C Denmark aims to obtain all its energy from non-fossil fuel sources by 2050.

D Recognizing contrasts

1 In the text, several sentences show contrasts using the words *but* and *however*. Find the sentences and complete the statements below in your own words.

    1 (Paragraph 1) *We may not know when this energy source will run out* _____

    2 (Paragraph 2) *We need a transformation in the way we obtain and use energy* _____

    3 (Paragraph 2) *This might be true* _____

2 Compare your answers with a partner.

E Making inferences

Which one of the following statements would the author probably disagree with? Circle the correct answer. Then compare your answer with a partner.

1 There is plenty of oil and coal in the ground. We shouldn't worry about developing renewable energy until they run out.

2 Although it is a renewable energy source, biofuel has some disadvantages.

3 The situation in Denmark is proof that renewable energy can replace much of our fossil fuel.

Discuss it

Work with a partner or in a small group. Ask and answer the questions below.

1 Look back at the ideas you highlighted. Are they the same? What are the differences?

2 The author suggests that when fossil fuels run out, the impact may be terrible. Which of the following events are likely to happen? Rank them on a scale of 1 to 5 (1 = very likely; 5 = very unlikely). Explain your ranking to your partners.

    Globalization will come to an end.   _____

    Gasoline prices will shoot up.   _____

    The cost of many products will rise.   _____

    The cost of food will increase dramatically.   _____

    Oil drilling in national parks will take place.   _____

4 Researching a topic

A Information gathering

Do you know where our energy comes from? The charts below shows the total global energy supply in 1973 and 2019, according to the type of energy. To compare different types of energy sources, the energy is converted into million tonnes of oil equivalent (Mtoe).

Work with a partner. One is Student A; one is Student B. Student A: look at the charts below. Student B: look at the charts on page 99. Ask your partner for the missing information and complete your chart.

Global Energy Sources

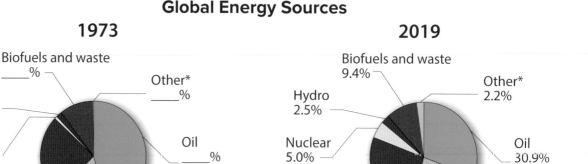

1973

Biofuels and waste _____%
Hydro _____%
Nuclear _____%
Coal _____%
Other* _____%
Oil _____%
Natural gas _____%

Total: _____ Mtoe

*Other includes wind, solar, and geothermal.

Source: IEA. License: CC BY 4.0

2019

Biofuels and waste 9.4%
Hydro 2.5%
Nuclear 5.0%
Coal 26.8%
Other* 2.2%
Oil 30.9%
Natural gas 23.2%

Total: 14,474 Mtoe

*Other includes wind, solar, and geothermal.

B Interpreting and reporting results

1 Work in small groups. Discuss the questions below.

1 What percentage of the world's energy comes from fossil fuels (oil, natural gas, and coal)?

2 How much energy did the world use in 1973 compared with 2019?

3 What other trends in global energy use can you see from comparing the charts? Can you explain them?

4 Apart from using green energy, we can also use less energy. Think of all the things you use that consume energy, such as air conditioners, vehicles, cell phones, and televisions. What things would you be willing to give up or use less of?

2 Share your group's ideas with the class.

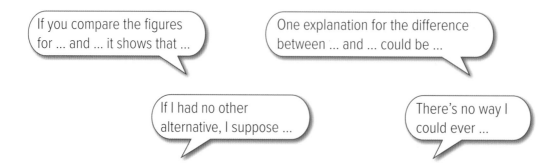

If you compare the figures for ... and ... it shows that ...

One explanation for the difference between ... and ... could be ...

If I had no other alternative, I suppose ...

There's no way I could ever ...

5 Critical thinking

A Fact or assumption?

Read the passage below, which is part of a speech made by the president of a solar panel manufacturing company.

Last year, we saw sales rise by 20 percent. This is good news, but unfortunately, high production costs and a fall in the value of the dollar mean that we had an overall loss of $525 million. However, the following five facts suggest that prospects are good.

1 Oil and gas prices will continue to climb. ____

2 Over the past five years, our factories have reduced costs by 30%. ____

3 People will pay more for solar power to protect the environment. ____

4 People will always reject nuclear power because it is too dangerous. ____

5 A 2021 study shows that 84% of young people were worried about global warming. ____

Three of the "facts" are actually assumptions. Work with a partner and decide which they are.

B Judging reasons

1 Decide who made the following statements and how believable they are. Rank each statement from 1 to 3 (1 = most believable; 3 = least believable).

Statement	Oil company executive	Solar panel company president	How believable 1–3
1 "Solar power will always be too expensive for most applications."			
2 "Solar power needs no maintenance and will pay for itself within 10 years."			
3 "New resources of oil and gas are being discovered every day."			
4 "We have to do our part to reduce CO_2 levels. Renewable energy is a moral choice."			

2 Compare your answers with a partner. Explain your choices.

C Writing

1 Write three facts and three assumptions about renewable energy. Don't write which is which. Then exchange papers with a partner. Decide which of your partner's sentences are facts and which are assumptions.

2 Tell your partner your answers. Do you agree with each other?

3 Choose one of your assumption sentences. Make that the topic sentence and write a short paragraph about renewable energy. Use your factual sentences to support your topic sentence.

Renewable Energy

D Presentation

1 Work in small groups. Your group has been invited to a world conference for young people to promote renewable energy. Discuss the questions below. Choose one person to make notes.

    1 What is the most appropriate renewable energy source for your country? Why?

    2 What will be the benefits of this type of energy?

    3 Are there any problems it will bring? What can be done to solve them?

2 Use your notes to prepare a three-minute presentation on why you think your energy source is most appropriate, its benefits, and challenges. Refer to the presentation tips on **pages 24** and below. Discuss and choose:

- a title for the presentation

- who will take notes

- two or three people who will give the presentation

3 Give your presentation to another group or to the class. Students who are listening should ask follow-up questions.

Openers

Have you ever considered ...?

I wonder how many people here know that ...

I'd like to begin with a quotation ...

I'd like to start by telling you a short story. After the massive earthquake in Japan in 2011 ...

TIP

Openers

The way you start a presentation is very important. Along with the conclusion, it is the part your audience will remember best. You need to quickly get people's attention and create interest in what you are going to say. Here are some ways you can do this:

- Ask a question
- Use a quotation
- State an interesting or surprising fact
- Tell a short story

66 Quotable quotes
Final thoughts . . . 99

I think so long as fossil fuels are cheap, people will use them and it will postpone a movement towards new technologies.

Paul Krugman
American economist

1 Do you think fossil fuels are too cheap?

2 Do we waste energy because fossil fuels are cheap? Give examples.

3 What other steps could governments take to promote renewable energy sources? Should renewable energy sources receive government subsidies?

Free Trade: Cheap Goods or Good Jobs?

"GLOBALISATION RISKY? HOW D'YOU MEAN?"

In this unit, you will:

- read an article about free trade in North America.
- read an article about the negative effects of free trade.
- discuss a case study regarding global trade.

1 Critical cartoons

A Building knowledge

Work with a partner or in a small group. Look at the information on this page and the cartoon. Discuss the questions below.

1 What does the term "globalization" mean?

2 Do you know of any countries working to globalize more?

3 What do you think might be some downsides to globalization?

4 What is the message of the cartoon? What is the connection to the unit topic?

> I think globalization refers to ...

> I think ... is making a lot of effort to globalize.

> I think one possible downside to globalization is ...

> The connection to the unit topic is ...

MEDIA link

The Pursuit (2019) is a documentary that shows how capitalism has decreased the number of people living in starvation since 1970 by more than 80%, and how it has made the US one of the richest nations on earth.

For additional media links, go to infocus-eltseries.com

A Skimming and scanning

1 Find and underline the keywords in the text. Try to guess their meanings.

Keywords

aspect	capitalist	implicit	likelihood	locally
migration	minimize	overhead	sustainable	undermine

Free Trade in North America

The topic of free trade in North America covers a broad range of issues and reflects a complex set of economic and social interests. It causes huge debate. One important aspect of the debate relates to the impact of free trade on local communities. Some argue that free trade agreements can help economic growth and job opportunities. Meanwhile, critics are concerned that such arrangements can undermine certain parts of the economy and weaken local industries. 5

The issue of sustainability is one important concern. Supporters of sustainable development emphasize the need to minimize the negative environmental impacts associated with trade activities. However, there are concerns that, in the pursuit of profits and lower overhead costs, companies may ignore ecological considerations. This could lead to activities that undermine the long-term health of the planet.

Another concern associated with free trade agreements relates to the potential effects of regulations. When 10 countries trade, they often need to adapt their regulations or laws to ensure smooth cross-border transactions. Critics worry that this may lead to compromising on important standards. They believe that such compromises could negatively impact public health, safety, or consumer rights.

At the local level, a key concern is the potential for the migration of jobs and industries. Capitalists state that businesses need to maximize profits. Critics worry that as companies pursue cheaper labor and operational costs, 15 the likelihood of job and industry relocations increases. This would seriously affect communities that rely on those

jobs or industries. It would minimize employment opportunities locally, make it hard for workers to earn enough money, and contribute to economic inequality. Also at the local level, communities worry that imported goods may be priced lower 20 than their own locally produced items. Such competition could weaken local industries, impacting the livelihoods of workers and farmers.

In conclusion, free trade in North America remains a much-debated topic. The outcomes implicit in free trade agreements 25 raise concerns about job migration, sustainability, regulatory laws, and local economic well-being. The challenge for policymakers and communities is to strike a sustainable balance between embracing the benefits of trade and protecting local interests. 30

2 Read the titles below. Which would also be a good title for the text? Circle A, B, or C. Then explain your answer to a partner.

A Concerns About Free Trade in North America

B The Global Benefits of Free Trade

C Winners and Losers in Free-Trade Agreements

B Words in context: concordances

1 Work with a partner. Below is a concordance for three of the keywords. Each group of three sentences has the same missing keyword. Find which word goes with each group.

> **concordance**
>
> a list of examples of a word or phrase as it occurs in a corpus (a collection of written or spoken language). Usually, one line shows one use of the word in context.

1	has changed" he says. "But it's just one	_____	of life, you know? You get a raise, but
	most experts say it's wrong to focus on one	_____	of your food intake: the right fats and
	this thing now," he says. "From a marketing	_____	, all the major sports convey that fans
2	would a seller take the additional risk	_____	in skipping the down payment? "It's a lot
	can borrow cheaply because of Uncle Sam's	_____	guarantee of their debt. More accounting
	conservative or progressive, left or right, the	_____	assumption being that when it comes to
3	along, have fun in the process but in all	_____	, you're not really going to see a dramatic
	have been shot, and the cast has in all	_____	moved on to other projects. If at that
	explain how companies pay to increase the	_____	their names will appear in searches

2 Make your own sentences using the keywords and compare them with a partner.

C Vocabulary building: word parts: *capital*   Example: *capitalist*

> **Words with *capital***
>
> capital   capital gain   capital punishment   capitalist

1 Use the words in the box to complete the sentences below. Try to guess the meaning of any words you don't know.

1 The Cold War was a time of tension between _____ and communist countries.

2 Because of the increase in property prices, Jinhee made a large _____ when she sold her house.

3 The restaurant failed because the owners lacked the _____ needed to buy modern equipment.

4 Most countries no longer have _____ because they believe it is against basic human rights.

2 Work with a partner. What do you think *capital* means? Write your guess below. Then check your answer with another partner.

I think *capital* means _____.

D Discussion dictation

1 Listen and write down the questions. Then discuss them in small groups.

1 _____ ?

2 _____ ?

3 _____ ?

2 Form new groups and compare your answers.

A Pre-reading

1 Quickly scan the text and circle the 10 keywords.

2 How does free trade affect unemployment rates in developed countries?

3 How can free trade affect the environment in developing countries?

B Reading

Read the text and check your answers to the pre-reading questions above. Then highlight an interesting idea in each paragraph.

Free Trade = No Bargain

We all enjoy a bargain. We all enjoy buying something at an unexpectedly low price. Perhaps we are briefly surprised at how goods can be imported from distant countries and yet sell for a remarkably
5 cheap price. But our surprise is soon forgotten in the satisfaction we feel in getting the bargain.

In reality, however, there are no bargains. The reason that goods can be obtained at such cheap prices is free trade. A couple of generations
10 ago, goods were manufactured and sold locally. British workers made British cars, and British car companies sold them to British consumers. French workers made cars in France, and these were sold to French consumers, and so on. With the growth
15 of multinational corporations and free trade, goods are increasingly manufactured where labor and overheads are cheaper. This migration of jobs from one country to another country with cheaper wages is called "outsourcing." Jobs are outsourced from
20 developed to developing countries. Implicit in this outsourcing of jobs is higher unemployment rates at home. This is why the bargain that we were so happy about is really no bargain: more people unemployed means more people receiving government support
25 and lower tax revenue for the government. The government spends more on welfare and unemployment payments, and at the same time, it receives less money in taxes. As a result, the likelihood is that everyone's taxes will rise. When
30 we consider the true cost of outsourcing, we should question the joy we felt at getting the bargain.

Another aspect of free trade and outsourcing is that the value of imports is likely to far exceed that of exports. The only way that this can continue is
35 by borrowing money from abroad or selling assets: goods, property, etc., to foreign buyers. But it is not sustainable—eventually, the credit will dry up, or the assets will run out. Some argue that free trade brings jobs to developing countries and so is a
40 positive force. This may be true, but most of these workers earn extremely low wages and often work in dangerous conditions. In developed countries, there are laws that protect workers from dangerous

materials and conditions. But workers in developing countries have few of these protections. Environmental protection laws in many developing countries are also relatively weak and so the local environment is exposed to damage.

If free trade is bad for both developed and developing countries, why has it become so widespread? The answer to this question is simple. First, we all enjoy the immediate satisfaction our bargain-priced outsourced goods bring. But free trade is also good, very good, for one participant: the multinational corporation. In a capitalist economy, corporations exist to make profits for their shareholders. In fact, corporations have a legal duty to maximize profits. In the world of free trade, a few multinational corporations make huge profits for their shareholders. Their executives also become extremely rich, earning tens of millions of dollars per year. At the same time, they pay nothing toward the lost jobs in the countries where they sell their goods and nothing toward the environmental damage and health risks in the countries where they make their goods. Corporations seek one thing: profit. They do this even if it means that the economy of a country is undermined.

JOB LOSS CEMETERY

It is time to minimize this destructive trend called free trade. It is time to stop the migration of jobs abroad and bring them home. We can do this by raising consciousness about the dangers of free trade. We can also do this by supporting local manufacturing. It is true, we might have to pay more for our goods, but when we calculate the total cost, we might discover that in the end, real bargains are local products made by local workers.

C Understanding the text

Read the questions below and circle the correct answers according to the text.

1 **GIST** What is this text mainly about?

    A Outsourcing of jobs

    B Environmental damage

    C Unrestricted trade

2 **MAIN IDEA** What is the main idea?

    A Free trade is good for corporations, but for most people it has negative effects.

    B Free trade results in cheaper prices for everyone.

    C Free trade creates jobs for people, especially in developing countries.

3 **DETAILS** In developed countries, free trade often results in …

    A increased exports.

    B increased imports.

    C increased imports and exports.

4 **DETAILS** Which of the following is NOT a common result of free trade?

    A Environmental damage

    B Fewer jobs in developed countries

    C Lower profits for corporations

D Cause and effect

Understanding why something happens (the cause) and what happens as a result (the effect) is an important reading skill. Read the statements below. Underline the words that represent the cause and circle the words that represent the effect.

1 Outsourcing results in people losing their jobs.

2 Tax revenue dropped by 10 percent because of unemployment.

3 The lack of regulations means that corporations can dump industrial waste into rivers.

4 Some companies care only about profits, so they don't worry about employee safety.

5 Local jobs can be created if we educate people about free trade.

E Making inferences

Which one of the following statements about free trade would the author disagree with?

1 "Globalization and free trade do spur economic growth, and they lead to lower prices on many goods." Robert Reich

2 "Where globalization means, as it so often does, that the rich and powerful now have new means to further enrich and empower themselves at the cost of the poorer and weaker, we have a responsibility to protest in the name of universal freedom." Nelson Mandela

3 "Free trade is very important if we respect equality among nations." Luiz Inacio Lula da Silva

4 "If you're totally illiterate and living on one dollar a day, the benefits of globalization never come to you." Jimmy Carter

Work with a partner or in a small group. Ask and answer the questions below.

1 Look back at the ideas you highlighted. Are they the same? What are the differences?

2 What kind of products are affected by free trade in your country? What outsourced products do you buy?

3 In your country, are there any industries that export most of their products? Do these industries employ many people?

④ Researching a topic

A Information gathering

Below is part of a graph. It shows the world's population, how much the world produces in a year, and the value of international trade. Work with a partner. One is Student A; one is Student B. Student A: use the table on **page 100**. Student B: use the table on **page 103**. Ask your partner for the missing information and complete the table.

B Interpreting and reporting results

1 Work in small groups. Using your tables, complete the graph. Then discuss the questions below.

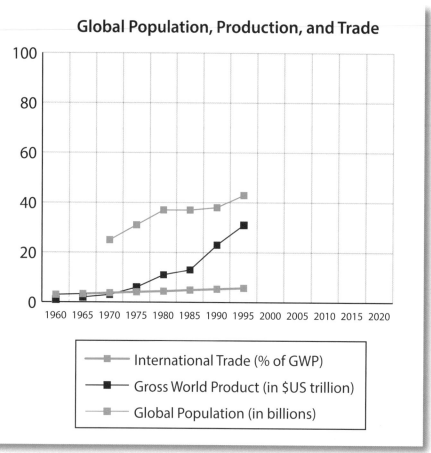

Global Population, Production, and Trade

Legend:
- International Trade (% of GWP)
- Gross World Product (in $US trillion)
- Global Population (in billions)

Source: World Bank 2023

1 How much has the global population grown in the last 50 years?

2 What has been the growth in gross world product in the last 50 years?

3 What has been the growth in international trade in the last 50 years?

4 What trends can you see from the data?

5 What reasons can you think of to explain these trends?

2 Share your group's ideas with the class. Groups who are listening should ask follow-up questions.

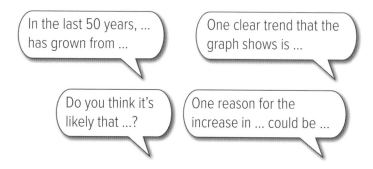

In the last 50 years, ... has grown from ...

One clear trend that the graph shows is ...

Do you think it's likely that ...?

One reason for the increase in ... could be ...

5 Critical thinking

A Clarifying statements

When you don't understand an idea clearly, you can ask people to clarify their statements—to explain them. Work with a partner. Take turns clarifying the following statements.

1 Free trade has a negative impact on children in developing countries.

2 Free trade is the solution to poverty in developing countries.

3 Capitalism is a dirty word for many intellectuals.

4 Free trade doesn't mean fair trade.

5 Consumers benefit from free trade and investment.

> Are you suggesting that ...?

> What do you mean by ...?

> I don't see the connection between ... and ...

> Can you give me an example of ...?

B Diagramming

Work in small groups. Below is a diagram showing the advantages and disadvantages of free trade. Add your own ideas to the map. Add boxes as necessary. You may want to refer to the texts on **pages 50** and **52** and other information in this unit.

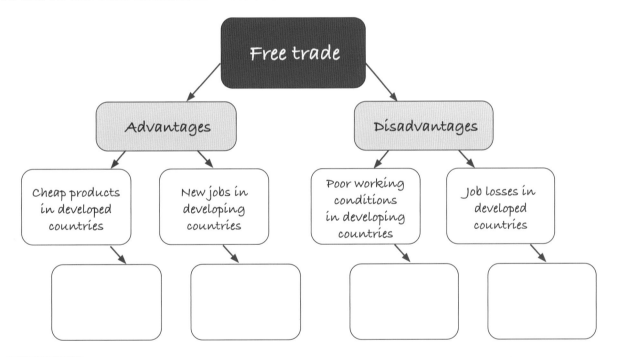

C Writing

Use the information in your diagram to write a paragraph that describes your opinion. The phrases and expressions below may help you.

When we discuss free trade, there are several important points to make.

One advantage/disadvantage of free trade is ...

Another factor that we must consider is ...

All in all, I believe that ...

You are a member of local government in a developing country with widespread poverty. A corporation from a developed country wants to build a factory in your city that will manufacture batteries. The details are below.

- The wages will be low, but 20 percent higher than the local average.
- Dangerous chemicals are involved, but the company promises to make the necessary safety precautions.
- The company has also offered to build an elementary school for local children.
- Local farmers are worried because pollution from the factory might affect their fields.
- Another town 100 kilometers away has offered to take the factory.

1 Work in small groups and make a list of benefits and problems relating to building the factory in your community. Then decide if your group supports or opposes the building of the factory. Refer to the texts on **pages 50** and **52** for ideas. Use the table to help organize your ideas.

	Benefits if the factory is built	Problems if the factory is built
Education		
Environment		
Jobs		

2 Join a group with the opposite conclusion. Share your ideas and discuss the issues. Remember to ask for clarification when needed.

We discussed the issues of ... and ...

Despite the benefits/problems this development would bring, we believe that ...

We are in favor of / against building the factory for these reasons. First ...

We think that the most important thing to bear in mind is ...

TIP

Summarizing key points

In a discussion, you need to be able to summarize the key points of your argument clearly. This helps your discussion partners understand what you think is most important. It also helps you organize your thoughts. Here are some phrases that may help you.

We feel that there are three key reasons for...

We have decided (not) to accept the offer for several reasons. First, ...

We think it comes down to two key issues. These are ...

3 Share your ideas with the class. Decide as a class whether or not you will accept the offer to build the factory.

"Quotable quotes
Final thoughts . . ."

While I believe firmly in open markets and free trade, I also believe an open market needs a level playing field.

Philip Hammond
British politician

1 What does Hammond mean by the term "level playing field"?

2 Can you think of some examples of "uneven playing fields" in your country?

3 How is this quote connected to the topic of this unit?

"I've decided to step down as CEO
so I can spend more time with my money."

In this unit, you will:

- read an article about a global financial crisis.
- read an article about capitalism and wealth.
- discuss a plan to provide social services to people in need.

1 Critical cartoons

A Building knowledge

Work with a partner or in a small group. Look at the information on this page and the cartoon. Discuss the questions below.

1 What do you know about how much money CEOs make? Check online.

2 Who are some famous CEOs or company owners? What do you know about them?

3 Do you think there should be limits on what CEOs earn?

4 What word in the caption makes this cartoon humorous? Why? What is the connection to the unit topic?

> I read that a lot of CEOs make ...

> One famous CEO in my country is ...

> In my opinion, there should(n't) be limits, because ...

> I think people expect the CEO to say ... not ...

MEDIA link

Saving Capitalism (2017) is a documentary with Robert Reich, a former US Secretary of Labor. It looks at America's widening income gap and its impact on the American economy, and explores the economic system from different viewpoints.

For additional media links, go to infocus-eltseries.com

2 Core vocabulary

A Skimming and scanning

1 Find and underline the keywords in the text. Try to guess their meanings.

Keywords

bundle	censor	illusion	liable	multinational
portrayal	recipe	sensible	trauma	unemployed

The Lehman Shock

On September 15, 2008, Lehman Brothers filed for the largest bankruptcy in American history. Although Lehman was an American company, the shock was felt all over the world because, like other multinational banks, they did business on a global scale.

The story began with a new way for banks to lend money to people to buy houses. Years ago, people had to pay a large deposit when they bought their houses. Then they were liable to the banks for the rest of the purchase price. But in 1999, changes in American banking laws took place. The banks were given the green light to combine different loans and sell these bundles of housing loans to investors. To increase profits further, banks began offering people 100 percent of the money for a new house. These were called "subprime loans." They were risky but very profitable. Banks also encouraged people to buy bigger houses than they could afford. Some critics compared American banks with Canadian ones, which had more sensible practices. They warned that this was a recipe for disaster. However, the big banks also funded the media, so the warnings were often censored or ignored. 5

10

Lehman Brothers bundled these subprime loans and sold them around the world. It knew how risky the bundles were, but it continued to promote them as risk-free investments. Business magazines, newspapers, and television shows repeated the company's claims. This portrayal by the media led many investors to buy these unsafe investments. 15

When the housing market broke down, many people tried to sell these bundles of subprime loans but discovered that "risk-free" was just an illusion. The bundles lost most of their value, and millions of people lost their savings. This resulted in a banking crisis that spread around the world. 20

Month after month, economic statistics got worse. More than nine million people in the United States lost their jobs over the next few years. These unemployed people couldn't pay their housing loans and tried to sell their houses. House prices fell by nearly 30 percent, while the stock market fell 50 percent. However, despite the trauma they caused to the economy, many of those responsible were not punished. These people, like those who worked at Lehman Brothers, were part of the "1 percent": the richest people in the world. Many believe that they did nothing wrong—they were simply pursuing the American Dream. 25

30

2 Read the titles below. Which would also be a good title for the text? Circle A, B, or C. Then explain your answer to a partner.

A The Collapse of the US Housing Market

B How the Global Financial Crisis Started

C Differences between American and Canadian Banks

B Words in context: collocations

collocations
common word combinations. For example, the noun *bankruptcy* is often found with the phrasal verb *file for*, as in *file for bankruptcy*.

1 We can use search engines, such as Google or Bing, to check the frequency of a specific phrase or collocation. To do this, put quotation marks (" ") around the phrase. Use a search engine to find the frequencies of the following collocations using three of the keywords.

Collocation	No. of results	Collocation	No. of results
1 **recipe** for disaster	_____	**recipe** for success	_____
2 **multinational** banks	_____	**multinational** corporations	_____
3 warnings were **censored**	_____	speech was **censored**	_____

2 Use the collocations above to make your own sentences. Use each keyword.

1 _____

2 _____

3 _____

C Vocabulary building: idioms   Example: *give the green light*

idiom
a group of words that together have a meaning that is different from the meanings of the separate words

1 Below are some idioms with the word *give*. Match each idiom to its meaning.

give someone a heads up	make a secret known to other people
give someone the benefit of the doubt	give permission for something to happen
give the game away	decide to believe someone even though you are unsure what they are saying is true
give the green light to something	tell someone that something is going to happen

2 Complete the sentences below with the correct idiom. Change the word forms as necessary.

1 Naomi said she was late for the meeting because the traffic was bad, and we _____.

2 The mayor _____ a new shopping mall.

3 Before the press conference, I was _____ that there would be important news.

4 Announcing the surprise party on Facebook really _____.

3 Now use the idioms to make your own sentences.

D Discussion dictation

1 Listen and write down the questions. Then discuss them in small groups.

1 _____ ?

2 _____ ?

3 _____ ?

2 Form new groups and compare your answers.

A Pre-reading

1 Quickly scan the text and circle the 10 keywords.

2 What is capitalism?

3 How has capitalism affected our standard of living over the last 100 years?

B Reading

Read the text and check your answers to the pre-reading questions above. Then highlight an interesting idea in each paragraph.

The Promotion of Wealth

Capitalism refers to an economic system in which there is private ownership of businesses and property. It is often contrasted with communism (or socialism), a political system in which the government
5 controls the production of all goods, no people profit from the work of others, and private ownership is strictly limited. Some people's portrayal of capitalism is negative: an unfair economic system in which a few people become rich from the exploitation of the labor
10 of the majority. Such people complain that there is too much income inequality and that the government should redistribute wealth to help the poor.

However, by any sensible measure, capitalism is a superior economic system. A small group of people
15 risk their wealth in businesses that improve the economy and make everyone wealthier. Without this small group of capitalists, most of us would face the trauma of economic depression and poverty. Compare the standard of living of an average person
20 of 100 years ago with that of an average person today. By any measure, whether health, education, or life expectancy, the modern person is better off thanks to capitalism.

Some people talk about Lehman Brothers and
25 complain about sales of worthless bundles of investments. On the whole, however, capitalism is fair. It rewards hard work and punishes laziness. History is full of rags-to-riches stories, in which poor people work hard and become wealthy. Capitalism
30 also promotes democracy. There are few nations with capitalist economic systems that are not democratic.

Unlike communism, capitalism promotes competition and discourages government
35 interference. This leads to efficiency and innovation. Market efficiency means that black markets are less likely to develop, and this reduces crime
40 and corruption. Internationally, capitalist countries usually develop deep connections with

each other and support free trade. Large corporations in such countries are often multinational. These economic ties promote policies that are beneficial to both sides. They also reduce conflict between nations.

An essential component of capitalism is private ownership. Wealth creation, along with property rights, brings many benefits. Take for example the environment: if there is no wealth, there is no money to pay for basic services, such as clean water and sewage systems. Without property rights, anyone could dump waste anywhere without fear of being punished. In a state with strict enforcement of property rights, dumping will be liable to civil and possibly criminal penalties. Communist countries may also have laws against pollution, but a private owner is more likely than a state to take action to protect property. Statistics show that the environment in capitalist countries is less polluted.

A final proof of the superiority of capitalism comes from history. The former Soviet Union and its associated communist countries are examples of an attempt by a central government to control markets and redistribute wealth. It didn't work, and the result was a poor standard of living compared with capitalist societies in democratic nations. The "workers' paradise" was an illusion: citizens of communist countries faced corruption, black markets, and shortages of commodities. There is a famous saying from this world: "We pretend to work, and the government pretends to pay us." Despite the boast of full employment in the Soviet Union, much of the population was effectively unemployed. Moreover, there was little freedom under the Soviet system. People lived in fear of the secret police, and speech was censored. The former Soviet Union and its associated communist countries are examples of an attempt by a central government to control markets and redistribute wealth. Such attempts are not a recipe for success. Capitalism may not be perfect, but no one has invented a better economic system.

C Understanding the text

Read the questions below and circle the correct answers according to the text.

1 GIST What is this text mainly about?
- **A** Free trade
- **B** Communism
- **C** Different economic models

2 MAIN IDEA What is the main idea?
- **A** Free trade removes inefficiency and creates wealth.
- **B** Capitalism is the best economic system.
- **C** Wealth leads to investments that benefit everyone.

3 DETAILS One result of a capitalist system is …
- **A** an increase in environmental pollution.
- **B** redistribution of wealth.
- **C** fewer conflicts between capitalist countries.

4 DETAILS Capitalism encourages …
- **A** the dumping of waste.
- **B** the protection of property rights.
- **C** environmental statistics.

D Cause and effect

Each statement below summarizes the author's ideas and follows a cause-and-effect pattern. Underline the words that represent the cause and circle the words that represent the effect.

1 Rich people invest in businesses that improve the economy.
2 Poor people become wealthy owing to hard work.
3 Competition leads to efficiency and innovation.
4 If there is no wealth, there is no money available for investment.
5 A poor standard of living comes from central government control.

E Making inferences

Which two of the following statements would the author disagree with?

1 "Capitalism works." Michael Bloomberg
2 "I am convinced that the path to a new, better, and possible world is not capitalism, the path is socialism" Hugo Chavez
3 "Capitalism is about adventurers who get harmed by their mistakes, not people who harm others with their mistakes." Nassim Nicholas Taleb
4 "The white man knows how to make everything, but he does not know how to distribute it." Sitting Bull
5 "Under capitalism each individual engages in economic planning" George Reisman

Discuss it

Work with a partner or in a small group. Ask and answer the questions below.

1 Look back at the ideas you highlighted. Are they the same? What are the differences?
2 The author believes that competition is an important part of capitalism. Should the following be run competitively by companies or non-competitively by the government? Why or why not?

- banks
- hospitals
- nuclear power plants
- police forces
- prisons
- schools
- space exploration
- the army

4 Researching a topic

A Information gathering

The table on the right gives information about inequality in the world.

The second column shows the Gini rank of the country from worst to best: the higher the number, the more equal the country.

The third column shows the Gini index, which measures the inequality in family income in a country on a scale from 0 to 1, but expressed as a percentage in the table on the right. If the income is more evenly distributed, the Gini index is lower. If rich people in the country have much higher incomes than the poor people, the Gini index is higher.

The fourth column shows the percent of income earned by the top 1% of earners.

Work with a partner. One is Student A; one is Student B. Student A: use the table on the right. Student B: use the table on **page 100**. Ask your partner for the missing information and complete the chart.

Inequality in the world			
Country	Gini rank	Gini index	National income earned by top 1%
Argentina		42.3	14.5%
Australia	116	34.3	
China	75		14%
Colombia		54.2	17.7%
India	99		22%
Indonesia	76	37.9	
Japan		32.9	12.9%
South Africa	1		19.3%
South Korea	144	31.4	
Sweden		29.3	10%
UK	111		13.4%
USA	54	41.5	

Sources: CIA World Factbook 2023; Our World In Data 2023

B Interpreting and reporting results

1 Work in small groups. Discuss the questions below.

   1 Which countries have the most equal and least equal societies? What do you know about these countries?

   2 Which countries have the highest concentration of income in the hands of the top 1 percent?

   3 In the graph below, match each point with the country it represents. What is the relationship between the Gini index and income earned by the top 1 percent?

   4 What do you find most surprising about the data?

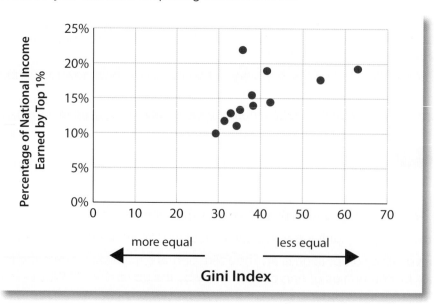

2 Share your group's ideas with the class.

> We think that ... has a high/low index because ...

> The graph shows that the relationship between wealth and income equality is ...

> One thing we found difficult to interpret about the data is ...

5 Critical thinking

A Clarifying statements

When you don't understand an idea clearly, you can ask people to clarify their statements—to explain them. Work with a partner. Take turns clarifying the following statements.

1 There's no such thing as a free lunch.

2 Capitalism promotes greed and inequality.

3 Without competition, we become lazy.

4 Welfare breeds dependence.

5 Capitalism means the death of the weak.

Can you explain what ... means?

I'm not clear why you say that ...

So are you implying that ...?

Do you mean to say ...?

B Judging reasons

1 Who do you think made the following statements? Check (✓) the boxes.

Statement	Capitalist	Socialist
1 "All schools should be privatized."		
2 "Employees perform best when their job security is guaranteed."		
3 "Everyone is entitled to a basic minimum wage."		
4 "Salaries should depend on staff performance."		
5 "Providing welfare to poor people just encourages them to be lazy."		
6 "Access to free or low-cost healthcare should be a human right."		

2 Compare your answers with a partner. Do you agree? Explain your choices. What is the connection between the statements and capitalism or socialism?

C Writing

1 Write three facts and three opinions about capitalism. Don't write which is which. Then exchange papers with a partner. Decide which of your partner's sentences are facts and which are opinions.

2 Tell your partner your answers. Do you agree?

3 Choose one of the statements in B above. Write a paragraph that expresses and explains your opinion about it. Try to connect it to your ideas about capitalism.

D Discussion

Economic recession in your country has resulted in an increase in the number of homeless and unemployed people. The number of people applying for welfare has increased dramatically. The Gini index is now one of the highest in the world. The president has proposed a plan to build facilities for the poor. The facilities would include hostels, healthcare clinics, and job-training centers. However, to finance the plan, income taxes will have to be raised by at least 15 percent. Citizens are divided between those who favor the president's plan and those who oppose it.

1 Form small groups. Half of the group supports the president's plan. The others oppose it. Discuss the issue. Before you begin:

Supporters Think of reasons to support the plan. What benefits will result if the plan is put in place?

Opponents Think of reasons to oppose the plan. What problems will result if the plan is put in place?

2 Share your ideas with the class. What is the majority viewpoint?

3 The country has agreed to adopt the president's plan. But government spending also has to be cut in order to fund it. Which of these things would you cut? Which wouldn't you cut? Why? Discuss the issues with your classmates. Ask and answer follow-up questions.

- Care facilities for the elderly
- Dental care
- Firefighters
- Healthcare
- High schools
- Police
- University scholarships for the poor
- Welfare payments to the poor

> If you think about all the homeless and unemployed, surely we have to ...

> I'm (not) in favor of raising taxes to pay for ... because ...

> I guess we could cut funding to ...

> There's no way we can cut ... because ...

TIP

Interrupting

In a discussion or debate, you may at times want to interrupt to say something important. Here are some expressions that you can use:

Excuse me for interrupting, but ...
Excuse me, but I really need to point out that ...
I'm sorry, but I don't think ...
That may be so, but I must add that ...

❝ Quotable quotes
Final thoughts . . . ❞

The end of democracy and the defeat of the American Revolution will occur when government falls into the hands of lending institutions and moneyed corporations.

Thomas Jefferson
Third president of the United States

1 Explain what you think Jefferson meant by this statement.

2 What do you think are the most important goals of a democratic government?

3 What are the main goals of corporations and banks? How might they be different from the goals of a democratic government?

Online Retailing: Disappearing Stores

"Excuse the interruption, but is now the right time for the surgeon to be looking to buy an automobile online?"

In this unit, you will:

- read an article about disappearing bookstores.
- read an article about the rise of online retail.
- discuss the effect the internet has had on the newspaper and travel industries.

1 Critical cartoons

A Building knowledge

Work with a partner or in a small group. Look at the information on this page and the cartoon. Discuss the questions below.

1 How often do you shop online? What kinds of things do you buy?

2 Are there any products you wouldn't buy online? Why?

3 Has online shopping had an effect in your country? Give examples.

4 What is the message of the cartoon? What is the connection to the unit topic?

> I buy stuff online …
> I usually get …

> I don't think I would ever buy … online.

> One way online shopping has changed things is …

> I think this cartoon is pointing out …

MEDIA link

Amazon Empire, The Rise and Reign of Jeff Bezos (2020) is a PBS documentary on how Jeff Bezos built Amazon from a small comany in his garage to one of the biggest and most successful online businesses in the world.

For additional media links, go to infocus-eltseries.com

2 Core vocabulary

A Skimming and scanning

1 Find and underline the keywords in the text. Try to guess their meanings.

Keywords

| behavioral | candidate | disadvantage | mall | revolutionary |
| simultaneously | specialty | strategic | susceptible | utility |

The Disappearing Bookstore

In 2010, the city of Laredo in the American state of Texas achieved a curious fame. It became known as the largest city in the United States without a bookstore. Since 2010, some small bookstores have opened in Laredo, but today, Laredo still has no major bookstores. Previously, like in most cities, there were a lot of bookstores in Laredo. Some bookstores had many different kinds of books, while others had a specialty like art or history. Bookstores owned by individuals who loved books competed with modern bookstores found in malls that only sold bestsellers. In Laredo,   **5**

most of these bookstores are now gone. This is of course less of a disadvantage now than in the past because of the internet. The internet has changed the book business in two basic ways. First, we can buy books online and have them delivered to our doors. Second, we can buy books in digital formats, which allow us to read   **10** the same book simultaneously on different devices, such as our computers, smartphones, or tablets.

Bookstores have been around for a long time, and booksellers have long been susceptible to both the economic climate and technological developments. The internet was not the first   **15** technology to transform the bookselling business. Around 1450, Gutenberg invented a printing press that changed the business in a radical way. Before Gutenberg, very few people could read. After Gutenberg, the availability of books brought about behavioral changes in society. People began to read for knowledge and entertainment. The bookstore was born.

The new way in which we can buy books is one example of the many changes that began in the 1990s with   **20** the growing use of the internet. Many newspapers and magazines changed their business models in order to survive this change. They saw the potential of the internet and created strategies to adapt their businesses. Other companies, however, questioned the utility of the internet for their business and paid no attention to the new marketplace. They backed the wrong horse, and most disappeared. They show that businesses that fail to plan for new technology will suffer, while those that make strategic plans based on new technologies are likely to grow. The   **25** latest candidate for a new technology that will require businesses to adapt is artificial intelligence. This technology will cause changes in business strategies that are as revolutionary as those caused by the internet.

2 Look at the pictures below. Which picture goes best with the text above? Circle A, B, or C. Then explain your answer to a partner.

A

B

C

B Words in context: concordances

1 Work with a partner. Below is a concordance for three of the keywords. Each group of three sentences has the same missing keyword. Find which word goes with each group.

> **concordance**
> a list of examples of a word or phrase as it occurs in a corpus (a collection of written or spoken language). Usually, one line shows one use of the word in context.

1 however, because there are multiple and _____ occurring processes that must be considered

caused by that. Just because two events occur _____ does not mean one causes the other.

and Corey were working on multiple dishes _____ while Jen was stirring only one risotto.

2 further the struggle for victory. Every _____ movement had to be supported

1848 and communism formed itself as a solid _____ movement in Russia in the early 1900s

Cold War world, the big ideas, the truly _____ concepts—space tourism, android domestic

3 says she knows a lot of the presidential _____ have been talking about the economy, but

that round, I knew that she would be a good _____ because of her qualifications, being a Pastry

guess that he would not be his party's _____ in the upcoming elections.

2 Make your own sentences using the keywords and compare them with a partner. Which meanings does your partner use?

C Vocabulary building: idioms   Example: *back the wrong horse*

1 Below are some idioms with the word *horse*. Match each idiom to its meaning.

back the wrong horse	a person who keeps their ability or skill secret
a dark horse	to hear something from someone who has direct knowledge of it
a one-horse race	to make a wrong decision and support someone or something that is later not successful
straight from the horse's mouth	a competition in which only one entrant has a real chance of winning

> **idiom**
> a group of words that together have a meaning that is different from the meanings of the separate words

2 Complete the sentences below with the correct idiom. Change the word forms as necessary.

1 I know it's true: I heard it _____.

2 In over 30 years of investing, he only occasionally _____. He is now worth millions.

3 This is probably going to be a boring election. It's really _____.

4 She is such _____. I never knew she had published a novel.

3 Now use the idioms to make your own sentences.

D Discussion dictation

1 Listen and write down the questions. Then discuss them in small groups.

1 _____ ?

2 _____ ?

3 _____ ?

2 Form new groups and compare your answers.

Reading skills

A Pre-reading

1 Quickly scan the text and circle the 10 keywords.

2 In what ways were stores from 130 years ago different from those of today?

3 What are some advantages of online shopping?

B Reading

Read the text and check your answers to the pre-reading questions above. Then highlight an interesting idea in each paragraph.

The End of the Store as We Know It

History is filled with examples of how technology transforms both our daily lives and the landscape of our towns and cities. Walking down Main Street 130 years ago, you would pass by stables for horses,
5 where gas stations stand today. There would be no supermarkets or convenience stores; instead, there would be many small shops, each one selling a limited range of products. Entering one of these shops, a modern time traveler would be surprised
10 to find that there was no self-service. Rather, the shopper would stand in front of a counter and order items one by one from the clerk on the other side. Imagine how much time this must have taken.

Introduced after World War II, supermarkets came
15 to dominate the retail space. They were more convenient because they carried a wide range of food items, and soon replaced most small shops. The spread of personal car ownership led to the growth of shopping malls, first in the United States
20 but later in much of the developed world. Malls were often located at the edge of town. This resulted in a behavioral change as shoppers came by car rather than on foot. More recently still, very large "big-box" stores began appearing at these shopping malls.
25 Usually, these stores either sell general merchandise or concentrate on a specialty, such as hardware, books, or electronics. Once again, progress provides the consumer with the benefits of a large range of goods and low prices.

30 Yet another transformation is now underway. In 1995, Amazon.com began an online bookstore. Customers could order books through the internet, and within a few days, they were delivered to the door. This proved very popular with
35 consumers for several reasons. Often prices were lower than those in conventional bookstores, and the range of titles in
40 stock was much greater than even the largest bookstore. Customers in some countries could also avoid sales tax.

Amazon soon expanded from books to music and other products, and other online retailers did the same. Today, it is possible to buy virtually anything online. As with online bookstores, prices are low, there is a huge range of goods, and consumers can avoid traveling and shopping in crowded stores. From the store's point of view, overheads such as rent, insurance, utilities, and staffing can be minimized.

Conventional stores are finding it harder and harder to compete with online retailers. They are operating at a disadvantage—they can't match the vast range of goods offered by online retailers, and their overheads mean that their prices will always be higher. Today, some shoppers enter conventional stores to try out a product. They may take photographs of products or product barcodes and then order the product from an online retailer such as Amazon. This is called "showrooming," and there are even smartphone applications that enable shoppers to simultaneously check and compare prices at several stores. Unsurprisingly, this makes conventional retailers very angry, but it seems that there is little that they can do about it.

Conventional retailers are victims of changing technologies that are driving shopping habits. This is nothing new—businesses have always been susceptible to change. It is part of the same process that saw small stores replaced by supermarkets and convenience stores. Although consumers can't obtain the same degree of personal service from an online retailer compared with a physical store, it seems that shoppers have already voted with their wallets and that online retailing is the way of the future.

In a strategic move to obtain even more market share, Amazon has built distribution centers close to many cities in the United States. These guarantee next-day or even same-day delivery of goods. The company has also entered the food retailing sector, and it is no doubt looking for other candidates for expansion. Revolutionary changes continue to impact the way we shop.

C Understanding the text

Read the questions below and circle the correct answers according to the text.

1 GIST What is this text mainly about?

    A Online shopping

    B The convenience of supermarkets

    C Changes in the way we shop

2 MAIN IDEA What is the main idea?

    A Small shops can't compete with large shops.

    B The way we shop changes over time.

    C Traditional bookstores will disappear.

3 DETAILS Showrooming angers traditional shop owners because …

    A customers buy online.

    B customers try out products.

    C customers take photographs of products.

4 DETAILS Amazon has built more distribution centers so that it can …

    A go into food retailing.

    B deliver to customers faster.

    C give more personal service.

D Identifying reasons

In the text, the author explains why shopping habits have changed or are changing. Match each summary of the author's reasons to the correct paragraph.

	Paragraph
1 Customers can look forward to online food shopping and same-day delivery.	_____
2 Online shopping provides advantages to both shoppers and online retailers.	_____
3 Supermarkets and big-box stores offer several advantages to shoppers.	_____
4 With online retailing, customers can easily compare prices among different retailers.	_____
5 Customers can choose from a wide range of goods and save money by buying products online.	_____

E Recognizing bias

1 Find and underline at least four phrases or sentences in the text that show the author's bias regarding online shopping. Write the line numbers below.

    1 Paragraph 2   Lines _____

    2 Paragraph 3   Lines _____

    3 Paragraph 4   Lines _____

    4 Paragraph 7   Lines _____

2 Compare your answers with a partner. Explain the reasons for your choices.

Discuss it

Work with a partner or in a small group. Ask and answer the questions below.

    1 Look back at the ideas you highlighted. Are they the same? What are the differences?

    2 Are products usually cheaper online than at a physical shop?

    3 Have you ever tried showrooming? What do you think of the idea?

    4 How can shop owners stop showrooming?

4 Researching a topic

A Information gathering

The chart below shows the percentage of the population who shop online in different countries. Work with a partner. One is Student A; one is Student B. Student A: use the table on **page 101**. Student B: use the table on **page 103**. Ask your partner for the missing information and complete the table. Then use the table to fill in the chart below with the names of countries.

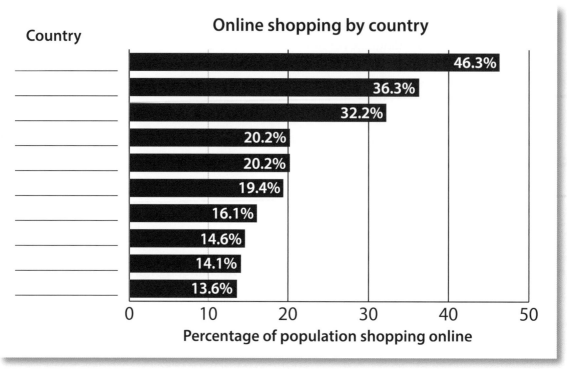

Source: Statista 2023

B Interpreting and reporting results

1 Work in small groups. Discuss the questions below.

   1 Which countries have the largest numbers of online shoppers?

   2 Which countries have the largest percentages of online shoppers?

   3 Which of the following factors most affect the popularity of online shopping? Why?

   • Advanced internet infrastructure

   • Widespread digital payment systems

   • Large population of internet users

   • Efficient transportation network

   What other factors might influence online shopping?

   4 If you were an online retailer, which countries would you invest in? Why?

2 Share your group's ideas with the class.

A Fact or assumption?

There are many different points of view on the subject of online shopping. Work with a partner and decide if the following statements are based on facts (F) or assumptions (A).

1 The majority of retail sales now occur online rather than in physical stores.   _____

2 AI-driven customer support chatbots are better than human customer service representatives.   _____

3 Online shopping results in reduced carbon emissions as compared to shopping in brick-and-mortar stores.   _____

4 The integration of AI in the retail sector will lead to the elimination of all cashier jobs within a decade.   _____

5 With the growth of online retail, local businesses are closing down at a higher rate than before the digital era.   _____

B Understanding reasoning

It is important to understand the different types of reasoning used in discussions. We studied four of these types in Unit 2. They are shown below. Read the definitions and then do the exercise that follows.

1 Jen and Steve are discussing online bookstores. Identify the types of reasoning they use and underline the words that support your answers.

> **Cause-and-effect reasoning** states why something happens (the cause) and what happens as a result (the effect).
>
> **Conditional reasoning** states that if one thing is true then another is also likely to be true.
>
> **Comparative reasoning** states that a conclusion can be drawn by comparing different ideas or situations.
>
> **Pros and cons reasoning** states arguments for and against a proposal.

Type of reasoning

Jen: I just got this book online. If I'd gone to the downtown bookstore, I would have had to order it. It would have taken a month and cost twice as much.   _____

Steve: We're lucky there still is a bookstore downtown. Bookstores are closing because of online book buying.   _____

Jen: But online bookstores are so much cheaper than traditional bookstores, and they have a much bigger selection.   _____

Steve: Well, you may save money and time, but you can't sit down in a chair with a cup of coffee in an online bookstore.   _____

2 Compare your answers with a partner.

C Writing

Write a paragraph about the effects of showrooming. Think of retail and online stores and their customers. Use the types of reasoning above.

> Shoppers are increasingly ...
>
> As a result, ...
>
> Although it's very difficult to ...
>
> One way the stores can try to fight back is by ...

D Presentation

1 You are going to discuss the effect the internet has had on the newspaper and travel industries in recent years. Work in small groups. Read the questions below and discuss them in your groups. Use the table to make notes.

1 How were the newspaper and travel industries 10 years ago?

2 How are they today?

3 Why have they changed?

Some things to think about:

- how to reach customers
- how to make a profit
- what advantages the internet provides

Industry	10 years ago	Now	Reasons for change
Newspaper			
Travel			

2 Prepare a short presentation around your answers. Decide who will take notes and two or three people who will give the presentation.

3 Give your presentation to the class. Remember to use the types of reasoning you have learned and structure your presentation according to the Tip on **page 24**.

Transitions

Up to now, we've looked at ... This brings us to ...

So far, we've talked about ... Now, let's ...

This leads us to our next point.

I'd now like to turn to the issue of ...

> **TIP**
>
> **Transition signals**
>
> A presentation is like a journey. It is important to provide signposts to help the listeners know where they are on the journey. Transitions are one kind of signpost. They link points you have already made to points you are going to make. Using transitions makes your presentation clearer and strengthens your arguments.

Quotable quotes
Final thoughts . . .

Lovers of print are simply confusing the plate for the food.

Douglas Adams
British writer

1 Why might someone love a printed book more than an electronic one? What is your opinion?

2 If print is the plate, then what is the food?

3 How will the technology affect other industries, for example, the medical industry? Try to give examples.

The Office of the Future

"Yes, I do usually work from home! How did you know?"

In this unit, you will:
- read an article about how COVID-19 changed the way we work.
- read an article about working from home.
- discuss the pros and cons of online learning.

1 Critical cartoons

A Building knowledge

Work with a partner or in a small group. Look at the information on this page and the cartoon. Discuss the questions below.

1 Would you like to work from home? Why or why not?

2 What are the advantages and disadvantages for the employee?

3 What basic rules should companies have for people who work from home?

4 What makes the cartoon humorous? What is the connection to the unit topic?

> I'm not sure I'd like to work from home every day, because …

> One advantage/disadvantage for the employee is …

> One rule for working from home would be …

> This cartoon is funny to me because …

MEDIA link

The future of jobs: Work from home, the office, or both? (2022) is a short 25-minute documentary from Al Jazeera that looks at working from home during the COVID lockdown, how it affected people, their productivity and happiness, and what the future holds for working from home.

For additional media links, go to infocus-eltseries.com

2 Core vocabulary

A Skimming and scanning

1 Find and underline the keywords in the text. Try to guess their meanings.

Keywords

bonus	converge	fraction	incidence	leisure
skip	slash	socialize	swap	tremendous

COVID-19: Reshaping the Work-from-Home Landscape

The outbreak of the COVID-19 pandemic led to a tremendous transformation in our professional lives. Almost overnight, many sectors, from finance to education, had to converge on one unexpected solution: working from home. This was not a mere shift, but a significant leap. It was driven by the high incidence of the virus, which pushed organizations to rethink their traditional operations.

At the onset, businesses slashed the number of in-office workers, letting only a fraction remain on site. 5
With the bonus of flexible schedules and the ability to manage their work environment, workers were easily persuaded. Moreover, this change meant that many no longer had to put up with traffic jams or crowded trains: they could skip the daily commute and enjoy more leisure time. Breakfast tables became desks, and formal suits were swapped for comfortable home clothes, at least from the waist down.

The education sector, too, underwent a huge change. Physical classrooms were quickly replaced with 10
digital platforms. The once-familiar sight of students rushing to class was replaced by the sound of logging into online sessions. However, not everything about this digital shift was smooth. Students missed out on the chance to socialize during breaks, and many teachers struggled to keep online students engaged.

But with these challenges came innovation. Many companies and educational institutions found unique 15
ways to integrate leisure and socializing into the digital world. Virtual coffee breaks, online team-building games, and digital classroom activities became common. For many, this was a chance to socialize, even if it was just through a screen.

However, the rapid push to remote work had its disadvantages. Many felt the strain from the lack of separation between their professional and personal lives. The inability to travel from the office to the 20
home meant that some people felt they were always at work. The incidence of stress grew, and the importance of taking breaks and separating work from leisure became clearer than ever.

In conclusion, the COVID-19 pandemic was not just a global crisis. It caused a significant shift in work culture and taught 25
us the importance of learning to adapt. As we look ahead, we can only guess how many of these changes will become permanent features in our working lives. One thing is for sure: the pandemic has left a permanent mark on how we work, learn, and socialize. 30

2 Read the titles below. Which would also be a good title for the text? Circle A, B, or C. Then explain your answer to a partner.

   A From Commutes to Clicks in a Pandemic

   B Challenges of Online Learning

   C Separating Work and Leisure

B Words in context: collocations

collocations
common word combinations.
For example, the adverb
fully is often found with the
verb *understand*, as in *fully*
understand.

1 We can use search engines, such as Google or Bing, to check the frequency of a specific phrase or collocation. To do this, put quotation marks (" ") around the phrase. Use a search engine to find the frequencies of the following collocations using three of the keywords.

Collocation	No. of results		Collocation	No. of results
1 **tremendous** potential	_____		**tremendous** loss	_____
2 employees **converge**	_____		people **converge**	_____
3 **slash** expenses	_____		**slash** costs	_____

2 **Use the collocations above to make your own sentences. Use each keyword.**

1 _____

2 _____

3 _____

C Vocabulary building: phrasal verbs   Example: *put up with*

Phrasal verbs with *put*

put someone off	put someone through
put something behind someone	put up with

1 Read the sentence in the text with the phrasal verb *put up with* (line 7) and the sentences below. Guess the meaning of each phrasal verb. Then compare them with a partner.

1 The report about its negative effects on health really put me off fast food.

2 I'm sorry to have to put you through this, but you need to know the truth.

3 Stefanos put his failure in the exam behind him and decided to try again.

2 **Use the phrasal verbs in the box to complete the sentences below.**

1 The company _____ all its mistakes _____ it and looked to the future.

2 Seeing so much corruption and greed really _____ me _____ politics.

3 Rita was unable to _____ her father's constant complaints.

4 Stan was _____ some tough questions at the job interview.

3 **Use the phrasal verbs to make your own sentences. Then compare them with a partner.**

D Discussion dictation

1 **Listen and write down the questions. Then discuss them in small groups.**

1 _____ ?

2 _____ ?

3 _____ ?

2 **Form new groups and compare your answers.**

A Pre-reading

1 Quickly scan the text and circle the 10 keywords.

2 How does working from home affect the environment?

3 What advantages are there for the employees?

B Reading

Read the text and check your answers to the pre-reading questions above. Then highlight an interesting idea in each paragraph.

Working from Home

Large amounts of time are spent each day commuting to and from work in the world's largest cities. Tokyo is perhaps the world leader, with an average one-way commuting time of 60 minutes,
5 and New York isn't far behind with 48 minutes. This represents a tremendous loss of potential productivity. If we base the working year at 250 days and the working day at eight hours, Tokyo workers spend the equivalent of more than 60
10 workdays per year commuting. And it isn't just a loss in productivity—there are other problems associated with commuting. If we could skip this daily commute and swap working at an office with working from home, great savings could be made.

15 First, there are environmental savings. CO_2 is of course emitted by cars and buses, but even if people use electric trains, CO_2 is a by-product of electricity generation. Fifteen million people converge on central Tokyo from the suburbs each day, and 1.2
20 million in Seoul. The infrastructure required to enable this movement of people is massive, and a huge amount of fossil fuel is consumed to support it.

It is not just the environment that suffers from the effects of commuting. People suffer, too. Road traffic
25 often slows to a crawl during rush hour, and at slow speeds, the engines of non-electric cars produce exhaust gases that are harmful to people's health. In many countries with public healthcare systems, these costs are passed on to the taxpayer. People also
30 suffer from stress, injury, and even death because of traffic accidents on their way to and from work.

Another cost is to the transportation network itself. Cities have to create and support transportation systems, which comes at great cost. And, increasingly in recent years, these systems need to be protected from terrorism. All these costs could be slashed if the majority of people worked from home.

There are other great advantages to be gained from working from home. One easy way to expand economic production is to have more people working. This happened following World War II, when many women entered the workforce. Today, for many developed countries, further expansion in this area is not possible. However, working from home offers a way for more people to join the workforce—stay-at-home parents, caregivers, people with disabilities, those living in rural or remote areas, and more. Not only are more people able to work, but also the talent pool is expanded. A further bonus is a reduction in the incidence of infectious diseases, such as influenza, and being unable to work. This is because people working from home aren't together physically at work and don't socialize after work. The direct cost of influenza has been estimated at $10.4 billion per year in the United States alone.

Currently, only a fraction of people work from home, but there are many direct advantages for employers to adopt a work-from-home system. First, there is a direct reduction in costs. Real estate costs can be reduced considerably if not all employees have to be physically present. With companies that do business internationally, having employees working in different time zones achieves further flexibility. In addition, research shows that employees who work from home have high job satisfaction because of increased leisure time, are less likely to change jobs, and are also highly productive. This reduces training expenses that employers otherwise might have to pay. Finally, surveys show that those who work from home are satisfied with lower salaries than employees who have to face a stressful commute to a noisy city each day.

All in all, working from home offers great benefits to employers and employees alike. And as technology advances even further, perhaps we can stop the massively inefficient movement of people into our cities and enjoy a future in which such employees become the majority.

C Understanding the text

Read the questions below and circle the correct answers according to the text.

1 GIST What is this text mainly about?

    A Remote work

    B Commuting to work

    C Protecting the environment

2 MAIN IDEA What is the main idea?

    A Working from home reduces costs for employers.

    B Large and expensive transportation networks are needed for commuters.

    C Working from home has many advantages.

3 DETAILS Which of the following is NOT an advantage of working from home?

    A Reduced levels of pollution

    B Reduced absence from work

    C Reduced flexibility

4 DETAILS Working from home can help the economy to grow because …

    A more people can join the workforce.

    B people work harder from home.

    C working from home doesn't use as much fossil fuel energy.

D Identifying reasons

In each paragraph of the text, the author provides a different point about the benefits of working from home. Match each benefit to the correct paragraph.

                                                               Paragraph

1 Working from home saves on healthcare and other costs.   _____

2 Working from home helps protect the environment.   _____

3 Working from home can increase productivity.   _____

4 Working from home reduces employer costs.   _____

5 Working from home expands the workforce.   _____

E Recognizing bias

1 Find and underline the phrases or sentences in the text that show the author's bias regarding working from home. Write the line numbers below.

    1 Paragraph 1   Lines _____

    2 Paragraph 4 (beginning on line 32)   Lines _____

    3 Paragraph 5 (beginning on line 38)   Lines _____

    4 Paragraph 6 (beginning on line 55)   Lines _____

    5 Paragraph 7 (beginning on line 71)   Lines _____

2 Compare your answers with a partner. Explain the reasons for your choices.

Discuss it

Work with a partner or in a small group. Ask and answer the questions below.

1 Look back at the ideas you highlighted. Are they the same? What are the differences?

2 What type of jobs are best suited to working from home? What jobs can't be done from home?

3 You want to persuade your boss to let you work from home. How many arguments in favor can you think of?

4 Researching a topic

A Information gathering

The table below shows the percentage of full-time employees in the US who have the opportunity to work completely remotely (Full-time remote) or partially remotely (Part-time remote), along with their educational level. Work with a partner. One is Student A; one is Student B. Student A: use the table below. Student B: use the table on page 101. Ask your partner for the missing information and complete your table.

Education level	Percentage of people offered the choice of working from home in the US	
	Full-time remote	Part-time remote
		21%
High school / Some college	29%	19%
		19%
Bachelor's degree	40%	26%
Advanced degree	45%	

Source: McKinsey American Opportunity Survey 2022

Now look at a chart that shows the percentage of people working from home by industry.

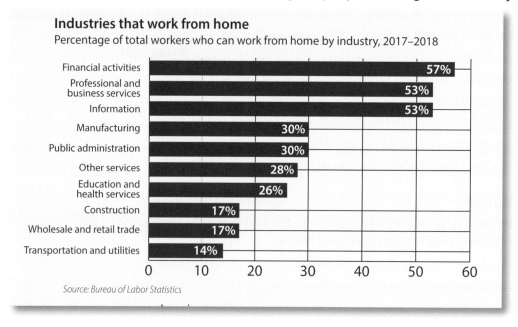

Industries that work from home
Percentage of total workers who can work from home by industry, 2017–2018

Financial activities 57%
Professional and business services 53%
Information 53%
Manufacturing 30%
Public administration 30%
Other services 28%
Education and health services 26%
Construction 17%
Wholesale and retail trade 17%
Transportation and utilities 14%

Source: Bureau of Labor Statistics

B Interpreting and reporting results

1 Work in small groups. Discuss the questions below.

 1 Which type of employer hires the largest number of people who work from home?

 2 Which educational background has the highest work-from-home percentage?

 3 What trends do you notice?

 4 If you were an employer, would you invest in equipment and training to support working from home?

 5 What information would you like to have about employees in order to learn more about working from home in the United States?

2 Share your group's ideas with the class.

> There seems to be a low percentage of people working from home in ...

> We were surprised at the percentage of people working from home in the ... sector because ...

> If we were an employer, we would probably (not) invest in ... because ...

5 Critical thinking

A Cause and effect

1 Work in small groups. Look back at the text on **page 76** and identify causes and effects relating to working from home and traditional commuting. Then decide in each case if the effect is a benefit or problem. Think about the effects on employers as well as employees. Write in the table below.

Cause	Effect	Benefit or problem
Traditional commuting		
Working from home		

2 In your groups, discuss what strategies could promote the benefits and reduce any problems associated with working from home.

3 Join another group and share your ideas.

B Judging reasons

At ABC English School, teachers work from home and interact with students through online video.

Work with a partner. Read ABC's advertisement and discuss the questions below.

1 What claims is the school making?

2 Which do you think are believable? Which are probably not? Why?

3 What additional questions could you ask ABC to decide if its claims are true or not?

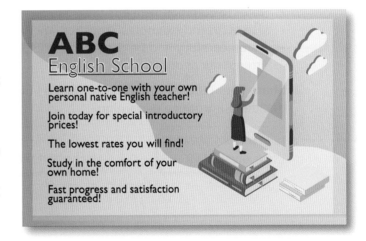

ABC
English School

Learn one-to-one with your own personal native English teacher!

Join today for special introductory prices!

The lowest rates you will find!

Study in the comfort of your own home!

Fast progress and satisfaction guaranteed!

C Writing

Write a paragraph about working from home. Structure it around the questions below.

1 How common is working from home?

2 What are its main advantages and disadvantages?

Working from home

D Role play and debate

Should our college reduce class time and introduce e-learning?
Like working from home in the workplace, e-learning and online teaching are becoming more common in colleges. Your college plans to introduce them. Here are the details.

- Class time will be reduced by 50 percent.
- Assignments and assessments will all be done online.
- 25 percent of teaching staff will remain in classrooms.
- 45 percent will be offered jobs as online teachers.
- 30 percent will lose their jobs.
- Remote teachers must accept a big cut in pay.

The following people are taking part in a debate over the plan.

Mimi Jarvis: Mimi is the vice president of the college and the developer of the new plan. She believes the plan will be popular among existing students and will attract new ones. She also believes that some teachers will find the new plan attractive.

Luis Ramirez: Luis is the academic director of the college. He believes the plan will lead to poor results both in student achievement and student assessment of the program. He also worries about teacher supervision and common standards.

Katie Reeves: Katie has been a teacher at the college for more than 10 years. She has been offered the chance to work from home as an online teacher. However, if she accepts, her pay will be cut by 50 percent. She also worries about losing regular contact with other teachers.

Jason Kim: Jason is a student at the college. He likes the idea of reduced class time but wonders if remote teachers can be effective teachers.

1 Work in small groups, ideally of four. Your teacher will ask you to be one of the characters. Debate the issues in your groups. Before you begin, think about your character and consider the points below. Refer to the information in this unit as necessary.

- Support your argument with examples.
- Refer to common sense.
- Use facts and examples, statistics, and expert opinion.
- Listen carefully and be prepared to respond to the arguments of others.

2 Share your ideas with the class. Take a vote. Does the class decide to introduce e-learning?

I'm sure it's obvious to everyone that ...

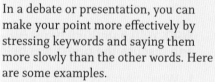
I'll give you an example of why I believe ...

According to a recent report about online learning ...

> **TIP**
>
> **Stressing keywords**
>
> In a debate or presentation, you can make your point more effectively by stressing keywords and saying them more slowly than the other words. Here are some examples.
>
> *I'm CERTAIN that everyone agrees with this.*
> *We are all against this proposal, and I'll give you THREE reasons why.*
> *This is one REALLY MAJOR benefit.*

66 Quotable quotes
Final thoughts . . . 99

Working from home means we can find a better balance between life and work. It also means we can be more productive in the comfort of our own space.

Richard Branson
British entrepreneur and founder of the Virgin Group

1 Do you think working from home will make you more productive?

2 What are the most important factors for you in job satisfaction? Why?

3 How important to you is your work-life balance?

Online Addiction: Too Much Fun?

Would you please turn that thing off and hibernate?

hibernate (v): to spend winter asleep

In this unit, you will:

- read an article about online addiction.
- read an article about online gaming.
- discuss the regulation of online gaming.

1 Critical cartoons

A Building knowledge

Work with a partner or in a small group. Look at the information on this page and the cartoon. Discuss the questions below.

1 How much time do you spend using your smartphone in a day?

2 What apps do you spend the most time using? Why?

3 Do you know anyone who seems addicted to using their phone? Do you think it is a problem?

4 What is the message of the cartoon? What is the connection to the unit topic?

> I think I probably spend around … on my phone most days.

> I spend the most time using …

> I have a friend who is always …

> This cartoon is a clever way to …

MEDIA link   *Web Junkie* (2013) is a documentary that follows three Chinese teenagers who are addicted to online gaming. They attend a clinic that uses behavioral techniques to help reconnect patients to reality.

For additional media links, go to infocus-eltseries.com

2 Core vocabulary

A Skimming and scanning

1 Find and underline the keywords in the text. Try to guess their meanings.

Keywords

allocate	epidemic	exponential	fatigue	inferior
intensive	interact	interfere	manipulate	realistic

Internet Addiction

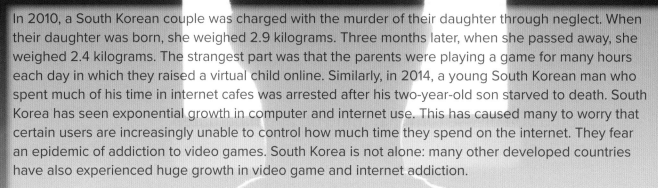

In 2010, a South Korean couple was charged with the murder of their daughter through neglect. When their daughter was born, she weighed 2.9 kilograms. Three months later, when she passed away, she weighed 2.4 kilograms. The strangest part was that the parents were playing a game for many hours each day in which they raised a virtual child online. Similarly, in 2014, a young South Korean man who spent much of his time in internet cafes was arrested after his two-year-old son starved to death. South   5
Korea has seen exponential growth in computer and internet use. This has caused many to worry that certain users are increasingly unable to control how much time they spend on the internet. They fear an epidemic of addiction to video games. South Korea is not alone: many other developed countries have also experienced huge growth in video game and internet addiction.

One of the main symptoms of an addiction is an inability to allocate a reasonable amount of time to an   10
activity. For example, people addicted to video games may play for 10 or more hours a day, often late into the night. The lack of sleep this causes can lead to fatigue and interfere with school, work, and social life. By not spending enough time on school or work, performance suffers. Often, people who suffer from addiction don't have a realistic view of how much time they actually spend on the activity. When asked, video game addicts may claim to play for only a few hours each day.   15

The people most at risk of developing an online addiction are those who are unhappy with their lives and who wish to escape through other activities. Frequently, the activity gives them something that is missing in their real lives. For example, after many weeks of intensive gameplay, they may achieve a level of success that is very different from reality. In real life, they might feel inferior to other people, but online they can feel they are superior to other players. In their real lives, they may not have the social   20
skills that help them interact with other people. But because it is much easier to manipulate a character in a game than a real human, they get a feeling of social control that they don't have outside the virtual world.

Like many things in life, playing video games and browsing the internet can be a source of great pleasure, but too much of a good thing is not usually best.   25

2 Read the statements below. Which best summarizes the text? Circle A, B, or C. Then explain your answer to a partner.

A Internet addiction is a growing problem around the world.

B The death of a baby was directly caused by internet addiction.

C Internet addiction has many causes and features.

B Words in context: concordances

1 Work with a partner. Below is a concordance for three of the keywords. Each group of three sentences has the same missing keyword. Find which word goes with each group.

> **concordance**
> a list of examples of a word or phrase as it occurs in a corpus (a collection of written or spoken language). Usually, one line shows one use of the word in context.

1

The media cannot be permitted to	_____	the outcome of a national election.
The image can also be easily	_____	on the computer to highlight or analyze
support for a philosophy comes from flawed analysis,	_____	data, altered history and magazine articles

2

lifestyles which have led to Britain's obesity	_____ .	The report is expected to highlight poor
since the first AIDS diagnosis in 1981. The	_____	's spread throughout the world continued
and child who is killed during this conflict, by bomb,	_____	and starvation, is just as much a casualty

3

The problems arise when their activities	_____	with the freedom of other hill users.
We firmly oppose any words or acts that	_____	in other countries' internal affairs" said
I can't imagine why you think you have any right to	_____	in my affairs

2 Make your own sentences using the keywords and compare them with your partner.

C Vocabulary building: phrasal verbs   Example: *pass away*

Words with *pass*

> pass away   pass out   pass over   pass up

1 Read the sentence in the text with the phrasal verb *pass away* (line 2) and the sentences below. Guess the meaning of each phrasal verb. Then compare them with a partner.

  1 I guess the reason Joao passed up the chance to appear on television is his shyness.

  2 That makes three times I've been passed over for promotion in this company!

  3 She was hit on the head and passed out.

2 Use the phrasal verbs in the box to complete the sentences below. Change the word form as necessary.

  1 After standing for two hours in the hot sun, the police officer _____.

  2 The boss _____ Hiro when recruiting a new manager.

  3 She _____ peacefully at the age of 96.

  4 Lucia _____ an opportunity to go to New York because she's afraid of flying.

3 Use the phrasal verbs to make your own sentences. Then compare them with a partner.

D Discussion dictation

1 Listen and write down the questions. Then discuss them in small groups.

  1 _____ ?

  2 _____ ?

  3 _____ ?

2 Form new groups and compare your answers.

A Pre-reading

1 Quickly scan the text and circle the 10 keywords.

2 How do you think the military might use video games?

3 What are some ways countries can regulate the sale of video games?

B Reading

Read the text and check your answers to the pre-reading questions above. Then highlight an interesting idea in each paragraph.

Fun, Popular, and Deadly

The video game industry is a multi-billion-dollar enterprise. A massive amount of resources are allocated to it, and from its beginning in the late 1970s, it has seen exponential growth. Reports on
5 the growth of the global market for video games predict high growth. A 2013 report predicted sales would grow from $67 billion in 2012 to $82 billion in 2017. That prediction was more than $20 billion short as actual sales in 2017 were $109 billion. A 2022
10 report predicted a market of $584 billion in 2030. But although this industry makes billions for companies, it comes at a cost. It is responsible for a huge loss of well-being in children, who make up many of its consumers. This cost consists of an increase in
15 violence, poor academic performance, bad health, and limited social skills.

From a young age, society explicitly and implicitly teaches us that violence against others is wrong and that murder is the worst form of violence. Therefore,
20 military systems around the world are faced with a problem. After a lifetime of social training that says that killing is wrong, how do they train their young soldiers to kill? The answer is that they do it through intensive training. And over the years, this training
25 has become more and more effective. Research shows that the willingness of soldiers to kill another human being in battle has increased in each war since World War I.

Over the last 20 years, military training methods
30 have increasingly used highly realistic video games. A frightening fact is that some of these video games are the same ones that are popular among young people. There is little
35 doubt that they have an influence, especially among young people, in committing violent acts. According to six
40 prominent US medical groups, violence on TV shows, movies, and video games leads children to become insensitive
45 and more likely to see violence as an acceptable way to resolve conflicts.

They are also more likely to have a tendency for violent and aggressive behavior later in life.

Violence is not the only negative outcome of video
50 games. Many young people become addicted to these games and spend hours playing them every day. They have little or no time for study, which leads to inferior academic performance. Moreover, they have no time for physical exercise, and this is one of the reasons for the
55 epidemic of child obesity. Gamers also develop physical problems from the fatigue and repetitive movement that video games require. Staring at a monitor for very long periods of time can even lead to seizures.

Another result of this addiction comes from the fact
60 that most video games are played alone. This interferes with the development of normal social skills. Some game players become loners who do not develop the social skills needed to be successful in school or in their careers. They may suffer mental problems and become
65 afraid to go out and interact with other people.

Despite all these negative consequences, game makers spend large sums on advertising because there is so much profit from games. Their aim is to manipulate children into persuading their parents to buy them
70 games. Parents often give in, sometimes spending money that should be used for food or education.

Some countries have passed laws controlling video games. Germany, for example, has a strict labeling system that restricts the selling of violent video games
75 to minors. China has many restrictions on what games minors can play and for how long. The video game industry in the United States, however, is mostly self-regulated, which is much
80 less effective. It seems clear that video games should be strictly controlled and mostly only played with parental supervision. A further
85 welcome development would be to legally force game makers to support independent studies that monitor the negative effects
90 of video games and look for ways to prevent these serious effects.

C Understanding the text

Read the questions below and circle the correct answers according to the text.

1 **GIST** What is this text mainly about?
   A Video game violence
   B Military training methods
   C Problems with video games

2 **MAIN IDEA** What is the main idea?
   A Video games harm minors and should be controlled.
   B Video games cause violent behavior in young people.
   C Parents spend too much money on video games for children.

3 **DETAILS** The military uses video games to ...
   A attract young people.
   B train young people.
   C entertain young people.

4 **DETAILS** Which of these effects of video games on young people is NOT mentioned by the author?
   A Obesity
   B Poor social skills
   C Poor eyesight

D Identifying reasons

In the text, the author explains how video games can have a negative effect. Match each summary of the author's reasons with the correct part of the text.

Lines

1 Violent entertainment makes people more likely to use violent ways to end arguments. _____

2 Video game players spend too much time on games. _____

3 Although video games make large profits for companies, they cause damage to young people. _____

E Prediction: concluding statements

Circle the statement that best fits the end of the final paragraph. Then compare your answers with a partner. Explain the reasons for your choice.

   A Parents and teachers, not corporations, should be responsible for children's exposure to violent video games.
   B Taking these simple steps will help reduce some of the problems related to video games.
   C Such video games have no educational qualities and should be banned.

Work with a partner or in a small group. Ask and answer the questions below.

1 Look back at the ideas you highlighted. Are they the same? What are the differences?

2 How can you recognize that somebody is addicted to gaming? What are the symptoms?

3 The text mainly discusses the problems of violent video games. Do you think the same problems apply to other forms of violent entertainment, such as movies or television? Why or why not?

4 Researching a topic

A Information gathering

Work with a partner. One is Student A; one is Student B. Student A: use the infographic below. Student B: use the infographic on **page 102**. Read the facts about video gaming. Ask your partner for the missing information and complete the infographic.

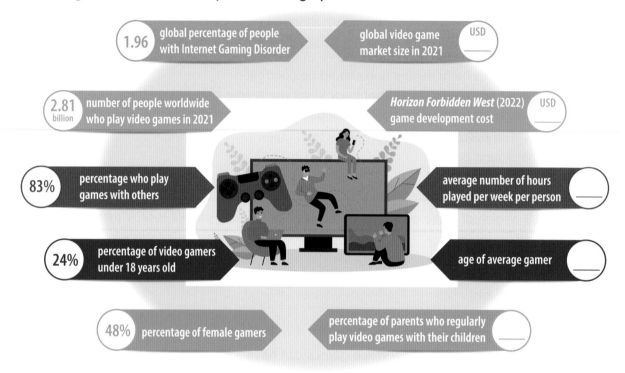

1.96 global percentage of people with Internet Gaming Disorder

global video game market size in 2021 — USD

2.81 billion number of people worldwide who play video games in 2021

Horizon Forbidden West (2022) game development cost — USD

83% percentage who play games with others

average number of hours played per week per person —

24% percentage of video gamers under 18 years old

age of average gamer —

48% percentage of female gamers

percentage of parents who regularly play video games with their children —

Sources: Entertainment Software Association, Entertainment Software Rating Board

	You	Your partner
1 Favorite game		
2 Number of hours per week spent playing		
3 Amount of money spent on games last year		

B Interpreting and reporting results

1 **Work in small groups. Discuss the questions below.**

  1 Which facts surprised you? Why?

  2 Which games are the most popular in the class? What makes them popular?

  3 How does your partner's playing time compare with the average?

  4 Do you think playing video games is an enjoyable leisure activity or a waste of time? Give reasons for your answer.

2 **Share your group's ideas with the class. What do most people in the class think about playing computer games?**

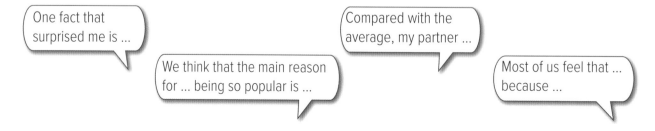

One fact that surprised me is …

We think that the main reason for … being so popular is …

Compared with the average, my partner …

Most of us feel that … because …

5 Critical thinking

A Decision-making

Look at the two summaries of articles about video games below. What decisions can be made based on this information? Match the decisions with the reasons and choose which decision is best in each case. Then compare your ideas with a partner. Explain your choices.

1 An article published in a video gaming magazine reported that playing first-person shooter video games increases hand-eye coordination as well as short-term memory.

Decision	Reason
1 Play more video games	because it is obviously biased and not credible.
2 Ignore the article	before making a decision.
3 Look for more evidence	to improve coordination and short-term memory.

2 An article in *Scientific American* reports on a study in an academic journal, which found that children between the ages of 14 and 16 who played violent video games showed more aggressive behavior and poor social skills.

Decision	Reason
1 Buy games with parental guidance controls	because all video games are bad for children.
2 Ignore the article	to limit the violence shown.
3 Sell your video games	because you haven't noticed an increase in violence among children.

B Understanding reasoning

1 A mother and her son have the following conversation about video games. What types of reasoning do they use? Identify the types and underline the words that support your answers. Refer to page 71 if necessary.

cause and effect	comparative	conditional	pros and cons

Type of reasoning

Mother: If your grades don't improve, I will throw out your computer. _____

Son: That might stop me playing games, but I won't be able to use the computer for schoolwork. _____

Mother: You're right, but I have no choice. Throwing out the computer means you can't waste time playing games. _____

2 Compare your answers with a partner.

C Writing

Write a letter to a newspaper complaining about the negative effects of video games on young people. Suggest that new laws are needed to control video game sales. In your letter, try to use at least two different types of reasoning. Then compare your paragraph with a partner.

D Role play and debate

Should video game sales be strictly regulated by the government?

The following people are taking part in a TV debate on the issue of video game sales to children.

Ada: mother of a 13-year-old son, Rusty. She thinks that Rusty spends far too much time playing video games. She has tried to limit his play, but she works part-time at a local restaurant two evenings a week. Ada thinks the government should strictly regulate the sale of video games.

Rusty: Ada's son. He thinks that he can balance his schoolwork and playing video games. He uses video games to relieve stress. He claims that he has learned a lot about history by playing these games.

Kelly: Rusty's math teacher. She notices that Rusty often falls asleep in class. She thinks that parents should be responsible for controlling which games children can play. She has noticed academic performance and social skills declining as video game playing increased.

Ajay: game developer. He is the creator of Brutal Thuggery, a popular but violent online game. Ajay thinks that the video game industry should regulate itself. He stresses that violent crime rates have never been lower.

1 Work in small groups, ideally of five. Your teacher will ask four of you to be the characters and one to be the TV presenter. Follow this structure:

   • The presenter introduces the topic.
   • The presenter invites each person to make a short statement with their point of view.
   • The four characters then debate the issues.
   • The presenter controls the discussion and makes sure that everybody contributes.

2 Share your ideas with the class. Take a vote. Do most classmates vote to regulate video game sales to children?

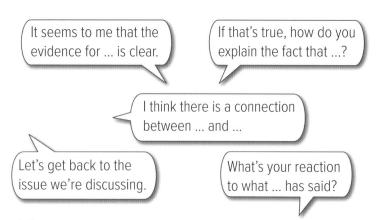

It seems to me that the evidence for ... is clear.

If that's true, how do you explain the fact that ...?

I think there is a connection between ... and ...

Let's get back to the issue we're discussing.

What's your reaction to what ... has said?

> **TIP**
>
> **Disagreeing**
>
> It's fine to disagree with someone, but it's important to be polite when you do so. You can do this in two ways:
>
>   1 Avoid being direct.
>   2 Give reasons for your opinion.
>
> These expressions may help you.
>
> *I understand what you are saying, but I don't agree, because ...*
> *I'm not sure you've thought about ...*
> *I see your point, but I'll tell you why I think differently.*

66 Quotable quotes
Final thoughts . . . 99

There are plenty of skills I've learned from playing video games. It's more interactive than watching TV, because there are problems to solve as you're using your brain.

Shaun White
American professional snowboarder and skateboarder

1 Are video games better than TV?

2 Fewer people are watching TV. Is this because of video games or other reasons?

3 Do you watch less TV than you used to? Why or why not?

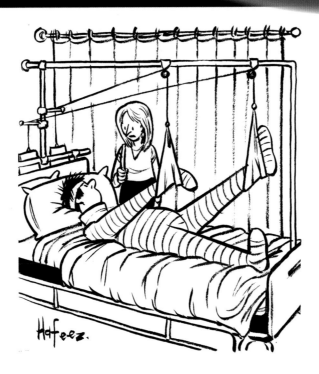

"If it's any consolation, the video went viral."

consolation (n): something that makes a negative situation better

In this unit, you will:
- read about the unexpected effects of social media.
- read an article about a connected world.
- discuss and present on the issues of cyberbullying.

1 Critical cartoons

A Building knowledge

Work with a partner or in a small group. Look at the information on this page and the cartoon. Discuss the questions below.

1 What social media sites do you use now? How about before?

2 What do you like about them? How often do you use them?

3 Is there anything you don't like about the sites you use? What?

4 What event does the cartoon show? What is the connection to the unit topic?

> I use several social media sites. For example, ...

> I really like ... because ...

> When I use ... I don't like the fact that ...

> I guess someone took a video of the man ...

 **MEDIA link**

The Social Dilemma (2020) is a documentary drama that explores the dangerous human impact of social networking. It features tech experts warning about their own creations.

For additional media links, go to infocus-eltseries.com

1 Find and underline the keywords in the text. Try to guess their meanings.

Keywords

communicative	demonstrator	facilitate	globalization	interrupt
media	onset	prejudice	productivity	regime

The Unexpected Effects of Social Media

The invention of the computer has led to and continues to lead to many changes in society. Predicting the future is difficult, and it is no surprise that some of the predictions about computer-based technology have been successful, while others have not. A few years before the onset of the computer age, Thomas Watson, president of IBM, said, "I think there is a world market for maybe five computers." This prediction was

5 obviously wrong. Computers allow humans to work much faster and do a lot more, so some predictions, such as an increase in business productivity, were easy. However, who could have predicted all the changes that Tim Berners-Lee's invention of HTML brought about? This simple program allowed computers to exchange data with each other and facilitate communication between humans and computers. It resulted in what we now call the World Wide Web. This communicative power of millions of computers linked together has led to

10 the globalization of business, culture, and many new media organizations, such as social media.

One prediction made about social media was that it would help bring about regime changes and a new era in democracy. In 2010, the Arab world was rocked by waves of demonstrators, demanding either change from their rulers or a change of rulers. This revolution became known as the Arab Spring. What role did modern technology have in facilitating this? The Tunisian government tried to suppress the messages of the

15 demonstrators, but it could not interrupt internet transmissions, so the messages spread to other Arab nations and around the world.

But this prediction did not come true. Governments realized that technology could challenge their power, and they acted. Many countries have departments to protect the country's national security. They use a variety of techniques to stop attacks on the country and disrupt their enemies' communications. Some people argue

20 that these government departments use similar techniques to impose limits on their own citizens—to try to control what they can read, hear, and even think about. One technique is to use people's prejudices as an excuse to suppress freedom of speech. For example, when governments label their opponents' messages as extreme, anti-democratic or containing misinformation, social media corporations are able to restrict the spread of this information. In this way, governments can suppress the messages of their opponents. However,

25 predicting whether such an approach will succeed over the long term is something that only the future will tell.

2 Read the statements below. Which best summarizes the text? Circle A, B, or C. Then explain your answer to a partner.

   A The internet has had many unexpected consequences.

   B Revolution has helped spread new social media around the world.

   C The internet and social media played a part in the Arab Spring.

B Words in context: collocations

"new regime"

Web   Shopping   Images   News
About 7,800,000 results (0.44 seconds)

collocations
common word combinations.
For example, the adjective
heavy is often found with the
noun *rain*, as in *heavy rain*.

1 We can use search engines, such as Google or Bing, to check the frequency of a specific phrase or collocation. To do this, put quotation marks (" ") around the phrase. Use a search engine to find the frequencies of the following collocations using three of the keywords.

Collocation	No. of results	Collocation	No. of results
1 hostile **regime**	_____	unfriendly **regime**	_____
2 gender **prejudice**	_____	racial **prejudice**	_____
3 social **media**	_____	news **media**	_____

2 **Use the collocations above to make your own sentences. Use each keyword.**

1 _____

2 _____

3 _____

C Vocabulary building: phrasal verbs   Example: *bring about*

Phrasal verbs with *bring*

bring about   bring down   bring out   bring up

1 Read the sentence in the text with the phrasal verb *bring about* (line 11) and the sentences below. Guess the meaning of each phrasal verb. Then compare them with a partner.

  1 We need to bring out better products if we want this company to survive.

  2 This scandal is so serious, it may well bring down the entire government.

  3 It's never a good idea to bring up the topic of money at the start of a job interview.

2 **Use the phrasal verbs in the box to complete the sentences below. Change the word forms as necessary.**

  1 The president was _____ by months of protest.

  2 The internet is _____ big changes in society.

  3 It is very hard to _____ that topic because he is so sensitive.

  4 In the last few years, many high-tech products have been _____.

3 **Use the phrasal verbs to make your own sentences. Then compare them with a partner.**

D Discussion dictation

1 Listen and write down the questions. Then discuss them in small groups.

1 _____ ?

2 _____ ?

3 _____ ?

2 **Form new groups and compare your answers.**

A Pre-reading

1 Quickly scan the text and circle the 10 keywords.

2 The invention of the printing press is one technology that has made it easier to spread information. What are some others?

3 What is one example of social media affecting the political process?

B Reading

Read the text and check your answers to the pre-reading questions above. Then highlight an interesting idea in each paragraph.

A Networked World

Historically, there have been four mass media revolutions. Each facilitated the spread of information in different forms and to progressively wider audiences. The first revolution was the development
5 of the printing press and oil-based inks in the fifteenth century, which allowed the mass printing of books. Before this time, books had been copied by hand. Extremely expensive and limited in subject matter at first, books became cheaper and wider
10 in scope over the following centuries. The second technology to affect mass communication was image recording. This began with photography in the 1830s and was followed by film in the late nineteenth century. The telegraph (1844) and telephone (1876)
15 came next, and the onset of radio and television brought about a fourth revolution in the first half of the twentieth century.

All these forms of communication that existed before the internet can be considered traditional media.
20 And with these media, there has been an increase in efficiency in terms of the number of consumers of information that can be reached per unit cost. This efficiency reached a peak with television. Over 3.9 billion people watched the television broadcasts of
25 the 2004 Summer Olympics; in 2008 this number peaked at 4.7 billion. However, all forms of traditional media share the fact that communication is top-down and one-way. In this respect, they are very different from social media, where the direction of
30 communication is virtually unlimited.

Social media is the fifth revolution. The term "social media" refers to the collection of internet-based communicative technologies that allow the spread of information among individuals and groups. Examples
35 are email, blogs, podcasts, wikis, and sites such as Twitter (now X), Facebook, YouTube, and Wikipedia. For the first time ever, large numbers of individuals have access to mass audiences. These technologies

are relatively young—Facebook began in 2004 and
Twitter in 2006—but already they are a dominant force in
spreading democracy and freedom around the world.

The first time that social media had a significant effect
on the democratic process was in the United States
2008 presidential election. The Democratic Party
candidate, Barack Obama, used a fusion of social
media to organize supporters and raise funds. His
campaign was able to raise a record $650 million and,
crucially, much of this money came from small individual
donations rather than corporations. This election also
saw people using smartphones and YouTube to monitor
voting. However, 15 years later, the "Twitter Files" have
revealed the many connections between social media
companies and government regimes. Correspondences
with government officials showed that social media
organizations were able to control, censor, and cancel
individuals who disagreed with official government
policies.

Some people argue that governments will always seek
to control the internet and social media, to prevent
the spread of information that is critical of those
governments. Over the long term, this is unlikely to
be successful because the social media technologies
that are used by demonstrators to protest government
policies are the same as those needed by corporations
to operate efficiently. There is a direct link between the
existence of web-based technologies and economic
productivity and development. I believe this means
that with increasing globalization, corporations are
much more likely to invest in countries in which these
technologies are unrestricted and avoid countries where
access to communication is restricted or interrupted.
Countries therefore have an economic incentive to
enable free, unrestricted access to information. This will
encourage the spread of freedom and democracy around
the world and lead to a decrease in conflict and prejudice
among peoples of the world.

C Understanding the text

Read the questions below and circle the correct answers according to the text.

1 **GIST** What is this text mainly about?
   A The print revolution
   B The spread of democracy
   C The impact of social media

2 **MAIN IDEA** What is the main idea?
   A Social media will lead to democracy and prosperity.
   B The US Democratic Party used social media to win an election.
   C The print revolution made books available to all.

3 **DETAILS** Before modern social media, what kind of media was able to reach the most people?
   A Radio
   B Television
   C Film

4 **DETAILS** Why will it be difficult for governments to completely restrict access to information?
   A Because corporations need free access to information
   B Because the internet changes quickly
   C Because the economy will grow

D Paraphrasing

The sentences below paraphrase parts of the text. In each case, find and underline the part of the text that is paraphrased.

		Lines
1	The Democratic Party used a mix of different social media to get people together and raise money.	_____
2	It has been suggested that some governments will try to restrict social media in order to prevent the spread of anti-government messages.	_____
3	The more internet-based networks exist, the more economic growth there will be.	_____

E Prediction: concluding statements

Circle the statement that best fits the end of the final paragraph. Then compare your answer with a partner. Explain the reasons for your choice.

   A Social media sites promote friendship among people all over the world.
   B Social media are much more than a tool for communication: they are a powerful way to spread social justice.
   C Although social media may cause many problems, they are beneficial to society on the whole.

Discuss it

Work with a partner or in a small group. Ask and answer the questions below.

1 Look back at the ideas you highlighted. Are they the same? What are the differences?

2 The text describes the positive impact of social media. What are some of the negative aspects? Some factors to consider are privacy, crime, and state control.

3 Overall, do you think there are more advantages or disadvantages to new social media? Why?

4 Researching a topic

A Information gathering

1 The table below shows the number of users of popular social media sites over time. Work with a partner. Student A: use the table below. Student B: use the table on page 102. Ask your partner for the missing information and complete the table.

Users of social media sites (in millions)									
Year	2006	2008	2010	2012	2014	2016	2018	2020	2022
Facebook	2	100	608	1,006	1,390		2,320		2,950
Instagram	0	0	0	1	200	500	1,000		2,270
LinkedIn	8	33	78	174	313		556	690	830
Pinterest	0	0	0	0		135		416	433
X	0	5	40	151	271	313		347	401
Snapchat	0	0	0	0	57	143	188		347
TikTok	0	0	0	0	0		133	700	

2 Use the information in your table to complete the graph of the number of social media site users over time and match the lines to the sites. Compare your graph with those of other pairs.

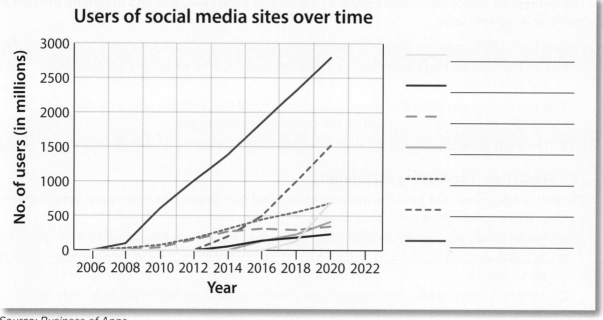

Source: Business of Apps

B Interpreting and reporting results

1 Work in small groups. Discuss the questions below.

1 How many of these sites do you know? What are their similarities and differences?

2 Which social media sites have the largest numbers of users?

3 What trends do you notice? What is surprising?

4 What explanations can you give for the data?

2 Share your group's ideas with the class.

> The most rapid increase/decrease can be seen with …

> We were surprised that the number of users rose from … to …

> We think that a key factor in a site's popularity is …

5 Critical thinking

A Decision-making

Two situations are described below, each with three possible decisions. Match the decisions with the reasons and choose which decision is best in each case. Then compare your ideas with a partner. Explain your choices.

1 You are the supervisor of 50 employees in an insurance company. Your information technology (IT) manager hands you a report that shows on average, employees are spending 58 minutes a day accessing social media sites.

Decision	Reason
1 Block access to the internet	to prevent employees from accessing them.
2 Block social media sites	so that employees know that they are being tracked.
3 Publish the report	because employees can access social media sites.

2 You are a parent of a 14-year-old girl who is a victim of cyberbullying. She has received messages from former friends and classmates calling her bad names. Some have even suggested that she commit suicide.

Decision	Reason
1 Ask your daughter for the password	to persuade them to tell their children to stop.
2 Call the parents of the bullies	because you think a crime has been committed.
3 Contact the police	so you can delete her social media account.

B Judging reasons

You are a friend of the parent in situation 2 above. You do some online research about cyberbullying and find the following sites. Read the short descriptions in the search results below. Which sites would you recommend? Compare them with a partner. Give reasons for your choice.

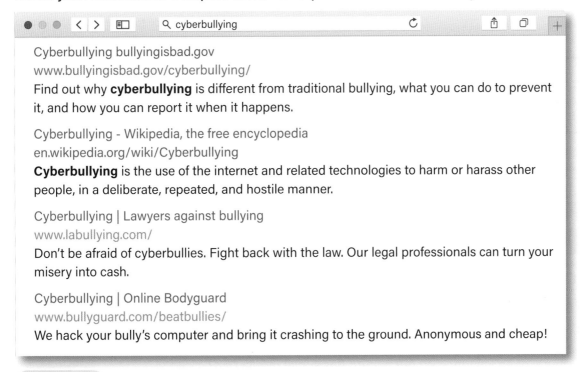

Cyberbullying bullyingisbad.gov
www.bullyingisbad.gov/cyberbullying/
Find out why **cyberbullying** is different from traditional bullying, what you can do to prevent it, and how you can report it when it happens.

Cyberbullying - Wikipedia, the free encyclopedia
en.wikipedia.org/wiki/Cyberbullying
Cyberbullying is the use of the internet and related technologies to harm or harass other people, in a deliberate, repeated, and hostile manner.

Cyberbullying | Lawyers against bullying
www.labullying.com/
Don't be afraid of cyberbullies. Fight back with the law. Our legal professionals can turn your misery into cash.

Cyberbullying | Online Bodyguard
www.bullyguard.com/beatbullies/
We hack your bully's computer and bring it crashing to the ground. Anonymous and cheap!

C Writing

Choose one of the situations in A above. In situation 1, write an email to the IT manager making a recommendation. In situation 2, as a parent of the girl, write a letter to a friend about what you intend to do.

D Presentation

1 Work in small groups. You have been asked to make a presentation to junior high school students. Your topic is cyberbullying and other anti-social online behavior, their effects, and how to prevent such behavior. Read the questions below and discuss them in your groups.

   1 What is cyberbullying?

   2 What technology is used by cyberbullies (email, cell phones, instant messaging, etc.)?

   3 Why do people become cyberbullies?

   4 Who are the victims?

   5 Who can the victims get in touch with for help?

   6 What is the best response?

   7 What are some other types of anti-social behavior carried out on the internet?

2 Prepare a short presentation to the class around your answers. If you can, include real cases that you have researched on the internet. Refer to the presentation tips on **pages 24, 48, 72, 80,** and below. Discuss and choose

   — a title for the presentation

   — who will take notes

   — who will prepare any visuals

   — two or three people who will give the presentation

3 Give your presentation to another group or to the class. Students who are listening should ask follow-up questions.

Closers

> I'd like to finish with the words of …

> Although a lot of work is still to be done, I believe things are improving and …

> So next time you hear about this issue, please try to …

> I hope that I'll be strong enough to help people who …

TIP

Closers

The way you end a presentation is very important. Along with the opening, it is the part your audience will remember best. It is your chance to summarize the key points and leave your audience with an interesting, memorable thought. Here are some ways you can do this:

- Give a personal message about the topic
- Give a recommendation or call for action
- Show a visual that connects to your message
- Give a quotation
- Express a hope for the future

66 Quotable quotes
Final thoughts … 99

Social media has infected the world with a sickening virus called vanity.

Kellie Elmore
American author and blogger

1 How much of an influence on our culture has social media had? Why do you think so?

2 In what way might vanity be connected with social media? Do you agree this is a sickness?

3 A recent study suggests that social media makes people unhappy. Why do you think using social media might make people unhappy?

Activities

Unit 1, page 6, Researching a topic

A Information gathering

Student B: use the table below. Ask your partner for the missing information and complete the table.

Global Gender Gap Index (total of 146 countries)					
Rank	Country	Score	Rank	Country	Score
146	Afghanistan	0.41	33	Mexico	0.77
	Argentina		116	Nepal	0.66
57	Brazil	0.73	2	Norway	0.88
30	Canada	0.77		Pakistan	0.58
107		0.68	12	Rwanda	0.79
3	Finland			Saudi Arabia	
1	Iceland	0.91	49	Singapore	0.74
127	India	0.64	105		0.68
87		0.70	18	Spain	0.79
	Ireland			Sweden	
79	Italy	0.71	48	Tanzania	0.74
125	Japan	0.65	129	Turkey	0.64
82	Lesotho	0.70	71	United Arab Emirates	0.71
102		0.68	43		0.75

Source: World Economic Forum, Global Gender Gap Index, 2023

Unit 2, page 14, Researching a topic

A Information gathering

Student B: use the table below. Ask your partner for the missing information and complete the table.

Marriage and divorce rates around the world			
Country	Marriage rate (per 1,000)	Divorce rate (per 1,000)	Marriages ending in divorce
Brazil	6.6	1.4	
China		3.2	44%
Egypt		1.9	17%
Iran	11.2		14%
Italy	3.2	1.5	
Japan		1.7	35%
Russia	5.3	3.9	
South Korea		2.2	47%
Turkey	6.8	1.7	
United States		2.3	45%

Source: Wikipedia

Unit 3, page 22, Researching a topic

A Information gathering

Student B: use the table below. Ask your partner for the missing information and complete the table.

Country	Total water resources per person per year (cubic meters)	Total consumption per person per year (cubic meters)
Canada		2,330
China	2,110	
Ireland		1,300
Israel	250	
Japan		1,380
Lebanon	1,070	2,110
Namibia	8,320	1,680
Portugal		2,510
Saudi Arabia	100	1,850
South Africa		1,260
South Korea	1,450	1,630
Spain	2,510	
Syria		2,110
UK	2,390	1,260
United Arab Emirates	30	
USA	9,850	2,840

Source: Food and Agriculture Organization of the United Nations (FAO)

Unit 4, page 30, Researching a topic

A Information gathering

Student B: use the table below. Ask your partner for the missing information and complete the table.

Fish facts					
Species	Atlantic cod	Atlantic halibut	Haddock	Sole	Bluefin tuna
Comments			Appears to be recovering	Has a very high risk of being sourced from unsustainable fisheries	Population down nearly 90 percent since 1970s
FAO status*	Depleted	Depleted		Over-exploited	
Tonnes of fish caught per year (1,000)					
1950			343	369	26
2000	940	4		261	
2010	952	6			49

Source: Food and Agriculture Organization of the United Nations(FAO)
*FAO status: under-exploited, moderately exploited, fully exploited, over-exploited, depleted (= shrinking population)

Unit 5, page 38, Researching a topic

A Information gathering

Student B: use the table below. Ask your partner for the missing information and complete the table.

Chornobyl and Fukushima Nuclear Accidents	Chornobyl	Fukushima
Number of deaths		2
Number of years plant was in operation before accident		40
Amount of nuclear fuel in plant (tonnes)		1,600
Number of people relocated		300,000
Highest level of radiation detected (mSv/hour)		73,000

Notes

• The radiation limit for nuclear power workers in the United States is 50 mSv/year.

• Approximately 50 percent of people exposed to 4,000 to 5,000 mSv over a short period will die within one month.

• The wind in Japan was blowing from west to east at the time of the accident. This was normal for the time of the year.

Unit 6, page 46, Researching a topic

A Information gathering

Student B: use the table below. Ask your partner for the missing information and complete the table.

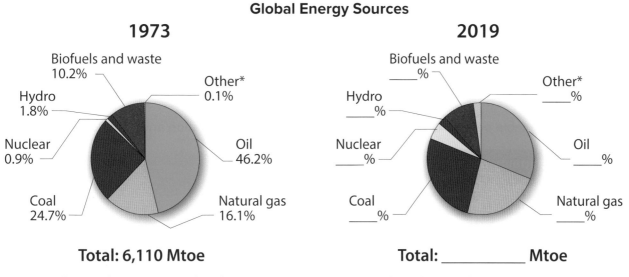

Global Energy Sources

1973

Biofuels and waste 10.2%
Hydro 1.8%
Nuclear 0.9%
Coal 24.7%
Other* 0.1%
Oil 46.2%
Natural gas 16.1%

Total: 6,110 Mtoe

*Other includes wind, solar, and geothermal.

2019

Biofuels and waste ____%
Hydro ____%
Nuclear ____%
Coal ____%
Other* ____%
Oil ____%
Natural gas ____%

Total: _____ Mtoe

*Other includes wind, solar, and geothermal.

Source: IEA. License: CC BY 4.0

Unit 7, page 54, Researching a topic

A Information gathering

Student A: use the table below. Ask your partner for the missing information and complete the table.

Global Population, Production, and Trade

Year	Global Population (in billions)	Gross World Product (in $US trillion)	International Trade (% of GWP)
1960		1	N/A
1965	3.3	2	N/A
1970	3.7		25
1975	4.1	6	31
1980	4.4	11	
1985	4.9	13	37
	5.3	23	38
1995	5.7		43
2000	6.1	34	51
2005	6.6	48	
2010	7.0	67	57
2015		75	56
	7.8	85	52

Source: World Bank 2023

Unit 8, page 62, Researching a topic

A Information gathering

Student B: use the table below. Ask your partner for the missing information and complete the table.

Inequality in the world			
Country	Gini rank	Gini index	National income earned by top 1%
Argentina	51	42.3	
Australia	116		11.1%
China		38.2	14%
Colombia	13		17.7%
India	99	35.7	
Indonesia		37.9	15.5%
Japan	132		12.9%
South Africa	1	63	
South Korea		31.4	11.8%
Sweden	159		10%
UK	111	35.1	
USA	54		19%

Sources: CIA World Factbook 2023; Our World In Data 2023

Unit 9, page 70, Researching a topic

A Information gathering

Student A: use the table below. Ask your partner for the missing information and complete the table.

Country	Population	Percentage of population shopping online
		46.3%
UK	67 million	
		32.2%
Denmark	6 million	
	274 million	20.2%
Norway	5.4 million	
		16.1%
Finland	5.5 million	
		14.1%
Canada	38 million	

Source: Statista 2023

Unit 10, page 78, Researching a topic

A Information gathering

Student B: use the table below. Ask your partner for the missing information and complete the table.

Education level	Percentage of people offered the choice of working from home	
	Full-time remote	Part-time remote
Less than high school	32%	
	29%	
Associate's degree	31%	19%
Bachelor's degree		
Advanced degree	45%	31%

Source: McKinsey American Opportunity Survey 2022

Unit 11, page 86, Researching a topic

A Information gathering

Student B: use the infographic below. Ask your partner for the missing information and complete the infographic.

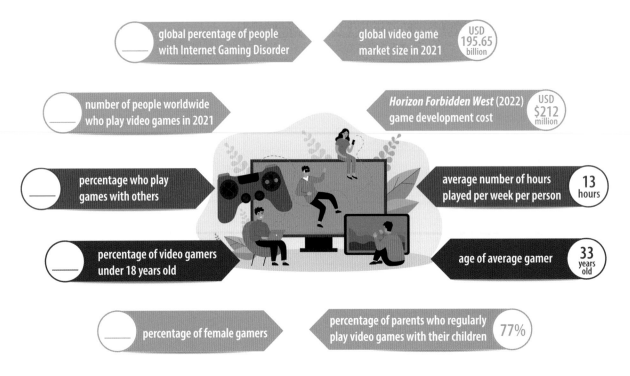

___ global percentage of people with Internet Gaming Disorder

global video game market size in 2021 — USD 195.65 billion

___ number of people worldwide who play video games in 2021

Horizon Forbidden West (2022) game development cost — USD $212 million

___ percentage who play games with others

average number of hours played per week per person — 13 hours

___ percentage of video gamers under 18 years old

age of average gamer — 33 years old

___ percentage of female gamers

percentage of parents who regularly play video games with their children — 77%

Sources: Entertainment Software Association, Entertainment Software Rating Board

Unit 12, page 94, Researching a topic

A Information gathering

Student B: use the table below. Ask your partner for the missing information and complete the table.

Users of social media sites (in millions)									
Year	2006	2008	2010	2012	2014	2016	2018	2020	2022
Facebook	2		608	1,006	1,390	1,860	2,320	2,800	
Instagram	0	0	0	1		500	1,000	1,520	2,270
LinkedIn	8	33	78	174	313	450	556		
Pinterest	0	0	0	0	0		231	416	433
X	0		40	151	271	313	298	347	
Snapchat	0	0	0	0		143	188	238	347
TikTok	0	0	0	0	0	0		700	1,366

Source: Business of Apps

Unit 7, page 54, Researching a topic

A Information gathering

Student B: use the table below. Ask your partner for the missing information and complete the table.

Global Population, Production, and Trade

Year	Global Population (in billions)	Gross World Product (in $US trillion)	International Trade (% of GWP)
1960	3.0	1	N/A
1965	3.3		N/A
1970	3.7	3	
1975	4.1	6	31
1980	4.4		37
1985	4.9	13	37
1990		23	38
1995	5.7	31	43
	6.1	34	51
2005	6.6		57
2010	7.0	67	
2015	7.5	75	56
2020	7.8		52

Source: World Bank 2023

Unit 9, page 70, Researching a topic

A Information gathering

Student B: use the table below. Ask your partner for the missing information and complete the table.

Country	Population	Percentage of population shopping online
China	1.4 billion	
		36.3%
South Korea	52 million	
	6 million	20.2%
Indonesia	274 million	
		19.4%
US	332 million	
		14.6%
Sweden	10.4 million	
		13.6%

Source: Statista 2023

Core vocabulary: keywords

Unit 1

authority

discrimination

distribution

dominant

ethical

justification

motive

scenario

traditionally

unstable

Unit 2

breakdown

compensate

elimination

formally

genetic(s)

goods

historically

legitimate

punishment

viable

Unit 3

consciousness

consumption

emergence

evident

minimal

namely

norm

prevalence

publish

ridiculous

Unit 4

ancestor

biodiversity

biologist

continent

degrade

rational

shallow

stabilize

treaty

widespread

Unit 5

accumulation

consensus

contrary

controversy

empirical

impact

neutral

rejection

statistically

transmission

Unit 6

bulk

exploit

finite

infinite

likewise

obtain

reliability

solar

transformation

utilize

Unit 7

aspect

capitalist

implicit

likelihood

locally

migration

minimize

overhead

sustainable

undermine

Unit 8

bundle

censor

illusion

liable

multinational

portrayal

recipe

sensible

trauma

unemployed

Unit 9

behavioral

candidate

disadvantage

mall

revolutionary

simultaneously

specialty

strategic

susceptible

utility

Unit 10

bonus

converge

fraction

incidence

leisure

skip

slash

socialize

swap

tremendous

Unit 11

allocate

epidemic

exponential

fatigue

inferior

intensive

interact

interfere

manipulate

realistic

Unit 12

communicative

demonstrator

facilitate

globalization

interrupt

media

onset

prejudice

productivity

regime

Alphabetical list

A
accumulation
allocate
ancestor
aspect
authority

B
behavioral
biodiversity
biologist
bonus
breakdown
bulk
bundle

C
candidate
capitalist
censor
communicative
compensate
consciousness
consensus
consumption
continent
contrary
controversy
converge

D
degrade
demonstrator
disadvantage
discrimination
distribution
dominant

E
elimination
emergence
empirical
epidemic
ethical
evident
exploit
exponential

F
facilitate
fatigue
finite
formally
fraction

G
genetic(s)
globalization
goods

H
historically

I
illusion
impact
implicit
incidence
inferior
infinite
intensive
interact
interfere
interrupt

J
justification

L
legitimate
leisure

liable
likelihood
likewise
locally

M
mall
manipulate
media
migration
minimal
minimize
motive
multinational

N
namely
neutral
norm

O
obtain
onset
overhead

P
portrayal
prejudice
prevalence
productivity
publish
punishment

R
rational
realistic
recipe
regime
rejection
reliability

revolutionary
ridiculous

S
scenario
sensible
shallow
simultaneously
skip
slash
socialize
solar
specialty
stabilize
statistically
strategic
susceptible
sustainable
swap

T
traditionally
transformation
transmission
trauma
treaty
tremendous

U
undermine
unemployed
unstable
utility
utilize

V
viable

W
widespread

Credits

In Focus Academic 1

2024年1月20日　初版第1刷発行
2024年2月20日　初版第2刷発行

著　者　Charles Browne
　　　　Brent Culligan
　　　　Joseph Phillips

発行者　　福 岡 正 人

発行所　　株式会社　金 星 堂

（〒101-0051）　東京都千代田区神田神保町 3-21
Tel　(03) 3263-3828（営業部）
　　　(03) 3263-3997（編集部）
Fax　(03) 3263-0716
https://www.kinsei-do.co.jp

編集担当　Richard Walker・Takahiro Imakado　　　Printed in Japan
印刷所・製本所／シナノ書籍印刷株式会社

ISBN978-4-7647-4195-9　　C1082